RESOURCEFUL EXFORMATION

some thoughts on the development
of resourcefulness in humans

francis laleman

Beyond Borders Publishing

Copyright © 2020 Francis Laleman bvba

All rights reserved

No part of this book may be reproduced, or stored in a retrieval system, or transmitted in any form or by any means, electronic, mechanical, photocopying, recording, or otherwise, without express written permission of the publisher.

Cover design by: Francis Laleman

contents

013 when empty means full
    a guest column by Georges Supreeth

017 exformation
029 exformation and learning design
055 the exformative facilitation method
077 exformative structures
135 exformation and coaching
159 the learning organisation

177 celebration

In this small collection of essays covering learning design, teaching, facilitation and coaching for individual and organisational development & growth, Francis Laleman makes a case for something new and fresh altogether.

This is not a manual, not a textbook, not a do-book. Rather, expect a series of transformative thoughts and exciting possibilities - for trainers, facilitators, (agile) coaches and assorted HR professionals.

Following up on ideas first introduced by the Japanese designer Kenya Hara, Francis brings the concept of ex-formation to the world of adult learning and organisations, merging it with ideas taken from Rabindranath Tagore, Herman Teirlinck, Paulo Freire, Augusto Boal and many more – thus transforming Hara's *communication method by making things unknown* into a social, artistic and educational movement, a model approach of exploration, discovery and learning, uniquely adapted to the field of HRD, or, as Francis would rather see it, the development of resourcefulness in human beings.

HRD Academy Belgium

disclaimer:
the ideas developed in the following chapters are the author's
and do not necessarily coincide with those of HRD Academy as an institution
(20200520)

*photo taken in Diesseits, an installation by Héctor Solari,
at Museo Juan Manuel Blanes, Montevideo, 2020.*

Francis Laleman was first a teacher of Sanskrit, the classical language of India, before he moved to social work, experimenting with non-conventional means of education among the destitute and the downtrodden – in urban slums, and on the paddy fields with landless farmers. Much of his educational approach was shaped in grassroots communities, before he turned to applying his work in HRD environments, in companies and organisations, from the early 1990s onwards.

Francis is a husband and a father, a painter and a writer. When he isn't travelling the world doing workshops, you are most likely to find him in the lushness of an English garden – or perhaps in a Japanese monastery.

kadam kadam par

with every step, the crossroads I see
are stretching their arms
and all the hundred roads that sprout
I wish to travel.

the stories that they keep set free
my dreams and open up
a myriad of opportunities
now ready to unravel.

now I'm ill at ease. I glee
that under every stone,
at every turn awaits a smile
eternity and lasting bliss.

yet hidden there beneath the scree
must be laments and grief
and pain and other poems
that I cannot miss.

I cannot choose. poor me.
I want it all. for all I know
the beauty of this life is
not of this and not of that.

I hesitate. I wail. I make a plea
to set me of this crossroads free,
to stop me at that door and let me
be in peace exactly where I'm at.

GM Muktibodh, 1917-1964

*with many liberties recreated in English
from the original Hindi*

the stories that they keep set free
- all pictures by the author, with Samsung GalaxyNote 8 -

when empty means full

a guest column
by George Supreeth (Ideasutra, Design for Social Impact)

Everybody has a plan until they get punched in the face.
#miketyson

The new disciple approached his famous Taoist master with awe. "Sir, what is the Tao?" he asked. The aged master cracked open an eyelid and said "When you're hungry, eat. When you're tired ... sleep."

"What?" asked the incredulous disciple "Isn't that what everybody does?"

"No" said the master. "People entertain a thousand desires when they should eat, they dream a thousand dreams when they should sleep."

Why do we do this? Why do organisations separate thinking from doing? Why do senior executives pretend to predict what will be, when they should first look around at what is?

One day, while we were discussing ideas, Francis came up with a funny word for this phenomenon. He called it *hubrisiness*. When senior executives forget that they perform within a complex adaptive system, where causality is non-linear and often invisible, hubrisiness occurs.

Hubrisiness separates thinking from doing and hubrisiness is why organisations get punched in the face.

Hubrisiness forgets that an organisation is an abstraction of industry. That the 'company' exists for the convenience of regulatory mechanisms. What an organisation really is, is wonder-

fully diverse, shared and networked cognition. The minds of a group of people who have come together in a unified cause.

True organisational learning leverages this network of minds, instead of stifling it. Like the Tao, it embraces diversity. A good learning model is empathetic to the human condition, it recognises that learning is a latticework of experiences. That modalities such as dance, music, theatre and painting are all sacred ways of learning because it understands that we thrive on metaphors and patterns. In this way, true learning accounts for exformation.

Hubrisiness is blind to all this. It treats machine learning and human learning the same way - as the filling of a container with information and rules, in the hopes that it will be assimilated.

I remember one incident when helping an organisation design a course for internal consultants. The head of L&D first drew a linear graph to indicate progression across learning modules. It was simple and articulate - a machine would have loved it, so we struck it out.

The second time, we redesigned learning progression as a spiral. In the new model, as the learner progresses outwards from the epicenter, she encounters familar concepts she learnt before, but in a new context each time. With each new outward blossoming of the spiral, exformation becomes an affordance, delighting the mind, as the learner recognises patterns she has encountered before. You see, it is in the space between the lines of the spiral where true learning occurs.

Like clay, when it is moulded into a bowl. It is the empty space that makes bowls useful.

George Supreeth
Bengaluru, January 2020

exformation

emptiness

Do I want to make empty mean full?

I like writing on a white page. I like working in an empty space.

An empty space has qualities of whiteness: where no colours are absorbed and everything is reflected towards the beholder's eyes.

Physics tell us that when all colours are reflected and nothing is absorbed, white is the result. Many people experience white as freedom. Perhaps because nothing of their perceived identities is being taken up by their surroundings. It all reflects back. Leaving one with a feeling of being left complete.

So, take an empty room and have all workshop participants enter at the same time, considering the doorway as the moment of birth and the opposite wall or corner, at the furthest possible distance, as the moment of "now."

Ask the participants to choose a location on their lifeline between birth and now – a place representing the phase in their lives in which they have learned the most, at the highest possible learning speed.

Take a minute-or-so away from this page, from this book. Consider the question for yourself. When was it that you were best equipped to learn, that you learned full speed, in the shortest possible timeframe?

(read on only when you are ready)

Some participants focus on the time of early adulthood, when they learned their trade. Others focus on the now, taking pride in experience gone through and wisdom acquired.

But most participants remain lingering near the door. And they are right. There will never again be such a time like the first thirty-or-so months of your life, when you learned essentially everything: breathing, walking, laughing, speaking, whatnot, ..., living.

Think of it. It turns out that the best learner is the smallest child.

The first thirty-or-so months.

What makes this timeframe so uniquely wonderful?

Let us see:

Perhaps, to a certain degree, we start off as a black object in a white room. All the colours and all the light of life is bouncing off from the surrounding whiteness and rolling back towards us, who absorb it all. This idea is similar to the one developed in Adlerian psychology, where the human being is entirely shaped and formed by her activities in, and relationships with the social and physical environment.

Perhaps, we are relatively free of preconceived ideas, of bias and other emerging constructs that will be limiting our minds as we go along and proceed in life. We are open. Not actively willing to learn, but learning, period.

Perhaps it is the case that at this point we are much less of a Self with capital S, or an Ego with uppercase E, than we will be at any given later time. The constructs of the Self have not yet taken form. There is no division, no border or wall separating hither from thither. From the activities-and-relationships idea in Adlerian psychology, it follows that the younger we are, the less of these activities and relationships are shaping us, or ultimately, the less limited we are by information and definitions being loaded upon us along the road.

Perhaps we don't need sentences? Perhaps we can do with words?

Open. Unlimited. Fragile. Newness. Sensorial. Embodied. Unknown. Unafraid. Spontaneous.

Perhaps the thirty-or-so first months of our lives is when from structures, shapes and forms, we derive new value and meaning.

Rather than giving shape or form to knowledge instilled upon us, and experiences offered, we are meeting shapes and forms as yet unfilled, and toy with them, attributing sense and sensitivity of our own and making them constituent parts of our ever-changing, always growing self.

RESOURCEFUL EXFORMATION

escher steps
Lisbon, Portugal, January 2017

the learning space

I cannot forget the first time I read Herman Teirlinck, a Belgian legend in theatrical education.

My feelings about his teachings were mixed, to say the least. I was young and somewhat theatrical in mind, but had little in common with established theatre as such. Rather, my heart was with the odd experimental street plays I co-created with social activist friends.

It was the time of Jerzy Grotowski's *poor theatre*, of Augusto Boal's *Theatre of the Oppressed*, of the *Indian People's Theatre Association* with Kaifi Azmi, of *Janam*, with my contemporary Safdar Hashmi, who would get killed while performing on the street in Delhi in 1989. I was a rebel.

Yet, from Teirlinck I took the idea of the *five carriers of creative expression* - space, plane, shape, time and word – in that order. [1]

Thus, space must come first, the medium into which we are born, the borderless box that we invade and co-create and make ours as we go along.

Right from the moment we start to exist, it is from the space around us that we learn the most. For this reason, when thinking of an ideal learning space, an environment in which we humans are best equipped to learn, develop and grow, I propose to rediscover the space enveloping us during the first thirty-or-so months of our lives, when space was boundless and free.

If, as we have seen, this is the period in which we learn best, I gather it would be valuable to try and keep recreating the conditions that allow us to do so.

Mainly, this would mean that we stop being the kind of adults that talk because we (think we) know, that give shape and form to the constructs we have in our minds – or, for that matter, in each other's mind.

Instead, we could try to grow up but remain young. In this case, we would always be like children. We would observe, eagerly open to understand, being proposed forms and shapes and structures in which we are free to inject meaning and value of our choice.

carriers

Like space, the other four of Teirlinck's *carriers of creative expression*, plane, shape, time and word, exist in perpetual dialogue between body and mind, senses and brain.

Teirlinck thought of these *carriers* as carriers of information: channels through which stuff, like thoughts and beliefs and ideas, can be caused to travel from one vessel, a creator or an artist, to another vessel, the audience.

In the following pages, I propose a different view. Through my practice, I have come to believe our *carriers* to be a whole lot more complex than the one-way highways suggested by the *carrier-of-information* concept.

Although I once started as an *informer*, one who knows and transfers his knowledge to the students or trainees who do not yet know, I have stopped all informative activities a long time ago – crossing the divide between being an informer and those who are to-be-informed – and joining the latter instead, creating one indivisible group of learners, learning with, from and among each other.

In cooperative togetherness, all five of Teirlinck's *carriers of creative expression* are richer, stronger, more pervasive, more transformative.

Space, which is now defined not just by the instructor but by all participants in the learning community.

The plane, a void waiting to be trodden, that sustains us and keeps us grounded and upright and ready to reach out to one another.

The plane – sometimes a sheet of white, allowing paint to be applied to it, invading its reflective power, urging it to leave its chrysalis of impermeability, setting it free, prodding it into absorption and refraction and enabling it to become both communicator and the recipient of meaning.

The plane, sometimes a screen with an empty page of Microsoft Word on it, waiting for letters to be typed and ideas to emerge and travel.

Shape, offering the possibility of form, of objects and bodies. Allowing contours and curves. Giving permission to the sensation of interaction and touch. And shivers of excitement.

Time, with direction and takt and beat and rhythm, allowing for noise that engulfs and permitting resonance that permeates.

Time, a process, the self-powered engine of change and growth and the cycle of life.

Time, with its infamous arrow. Creator of impermanence, uncertainty, complexity.

Time, eternity.

And word.

Good old word.

The words printed on the plane of this page. Being read and digested by you, a mindful shape, impermanent, through time, a process of eternity. Words, collated in a book or on the screen of a notebook, a volume that you are carrying with you at this very moment.

Words that never say enough.

Words that are glued in form, in grammar and spelling and syntax.

And yet never say enough.

information

So I stopped being an informer.

Information is an activity of making things known.

It flows from the one who knows to the one who doesn't. It is plenty of *in*-form, provided with a distinctive, not always altogether wholesome goal.

Think of a lecturer. Who *in*-fuses the minds and bodies of the audience with stuff already known by herself.

The lecturer, who creates shapes and words for the ideas in one brain, his own, and sends them off packing, to be instilled in the brains of the others.

The teacher, who creates words and shapes and time for the skills and craftspersonship in one body, her own, and sends it off packing, to be instilled in the bodies of the others.

exformation

Exformation is an activity of making things unknown.

Exformation flows hither and thither, deconstructing what we already know and opening up a space and a plane and a volume and a time and a word, to be continuously reconstructed and replenished with new meaning – creating new spaces and planes and volumes and times and words as we go along.

Think of a gentle cooperative facilitator. Who listens and observes and creates a holding space in which conversations take place, meaning is explored, interpretations are shared, applications imagined.

Exformation.

Exformation is where learning happens.

exformation with shapes of glass
The Glass Factory, Emmaboda, Sweden, July 2019

exformation and learning design

turning instruction inside out

When designing learning tracks, we should stop defining what we do as *instructional design*. Instruction implies information and information implies a mere *transmission* of the already known.

When designing learning tracks, we should consider experiencing what we do as *ex-structional design*. Ex-struction implies exformation and exformation implies a *transformation* of the already known into the possibilities enshrined in the as yet unknown.

RESOURCEFUL EXFORMATION

exstruction
Raketenstation Hombroich, Neuss, Germany, November 2018

learning objectives

When designing learning tracks, we should stop working onwards from *learning objectives*.

Whose objectives are they anyway?

The answer is that learning objectives are defined not by the learner, but by someone representing power. Power over the one that learns. Power by entitlement over knowledge already gained. Power over a status-quo. Power over the fact that *thou shalt learn what I do tell you*.

Learning objectives are artefacts of information.

learning needs

Likewise, we should stop working onwards from *learning needs*.

What are learning needs anyway?

There is ample discussion on whether or not what we learn in schools and education is *needed* or even useful. Voices are raised, claiming that learning which is of no use should be abolished.

I don't know about this.

I am very happy that I once learned how to make a swing and attach it safely to the branch of a fir tree in my parents' woods. I will always remember how an eccentric friend of the father of a friend of mine once taught me how to catch a fish with my bare hands and feel it wriggle and go desperate for life, and then release it back into the forest pond.

Stuff does not need to be needed or need to be useful for it to be meaningful.

I never needed nor *used* my knowledge of this-or-that Bach Cantata or Mahler's second symphony.

I never *used* my knowledge of vector mathematics and I never *used* my remembering most of Marcus Tullius Cicero's first speech against Catiline or The Cloud Messenger by Kalidasa.

And yet – all these subjects have made me into the person I am. All these subjects have a lasting impact on my "performance" as a human being.

All these subjects have become my resources.

All these subjects contribute to my resourcefulness.

All these subjects do matter in the life, including work, and the conversations I share with others.

needs in time

Of course I do acknowledge that within the constraints of an organisation, a certain learning is needed at a certain moment in time – in order for the people in the organisation to be apt and able to perform certain activities and conversations that create the value that is promised by the organisation to its customers.

Particular needs on a particular moment in time are okay.

But more than a moment, time is a process, the self-powered engine of change and growth and the cycle of life, the creator of impermanence, uncertainty and complexity.

Not for long can time be frozen in space and shape, an empty vessel waiting to be filled with *just-in-times*.

Time is not a vessel. Time is a flow. And where time is permitted its role as part of the equation, learning becomes continuous and flowing, like time itself.

Training is a vessel being filled. *Learning* is a river flowing by.

Filling a vessel is information, in a permanent illusion of the certainty of a moment.

Enabling a river to flow is exformation, embracing the uncertainties of adaptation, evolution and growth.

flow on rocks
Maruo Falls, Kirishima, Japan, August 2018

user stories

Instead of learning objectives and learning needs, what matters is the stories of the learners, as told by the learners, prior to shaping and forming and boxing and planning anything at all.

In software development and product management, the *user stories* of today are informal, natural language descriptions of one or more features of a software system. As such, user stories have a very particular grammar and format.

But I have a different spectrum in mind, broader in one way, more particular in another.

In fact, user stories have been around for a very long time. I first learned about user stories as a student at university, in the context of Buddhist philosophy.

As a bodhisattva, someone having an affordance for Buddhahood, I need to deploy bodhicitta (a buddha mindset) in order to be capable of acting for the benefit of all sentient beings.

User stories are strong but powerful creatures. They permit the learner to be in charge of her own situation and express a keenness to learn in her very own particular context and situation.

As a mother, I am keen to learn just enough algebra so that I can help my daughter with homework.

As an operator, I am keen on knowing just enough about the functionalities of the installation I operate, in order to permit myself the freedom to feel safe and content throughout my shift.

Unlike learning objectives and learning needs, learner's user stories exist in a space of dazzling possibilities, a choice of colours on an boundless plane, a range of unknown shapes and volumes and forms, a swiftly rolling river of time, with waves always changing and droplets of water endlessly passing by, tirelessly recreating the riverbed where words, like pebbles and grains of sand, keep forming new constellations of meanings never imagined before.

As a Scrum Master, I am keen on developing my drawing skills, in order to be able to better visualize the ideas emerging in the course of a retrospective and make them last as stories to learn from.

Learner's user stories always aim for a learner to become a better version of herself.

As a gardener, I am keen on improving my pruning skills in order to provide more blossom on the trees, for them to thrive and for the garden visitors to enjoy.

Learner's user stories always connect the learner to his environment, creating learning opportunities through dialogue and relationships.

Learner's user stories never have a pre-defined answer. Instead, they express a willingness to learn, an openness to explore, a journey towards the as yet unknown, the as yet unpractised. Learner's user stories are artefacts of exformation.

exformative conversations with portraits in a gallery
= onuitgesproken: untold, unsaid, there is more to say =
a Michel Van Dousselaere, Irma Wijsman & Stephan Vanfleteren exhibition
Museum Dr Guislain, Gent, Belgium, December 2019

diversity

But having stories is not enough. Stories need to be shared. With a group of peers as wide and diverse as can be.

Monologue, like hierarchy, is a building block of classical lecturing and *giving training* – where information is passed from the known to the to-be-knowing.

Through dialogue and relationships, on the other hand, the unknown is explored.

Dialogue and relationships are the keystones of exformative learning.

All too often, in an environment of living and working together, where dialogue and relationships matter, where wholesome dialogues and relationships are the very condition of success - the diversity aspect of dialogues and relationships is seen as a difficulty to overcome, a problem to be solved.

Diversity is assumed to kindle disagreement, generate dissent, enforce us-versus-them-thinking. Diversity is seen as an un-dialoguer, an un-relater.

Diversity, forever the dreaded *difficultivator* of everything we want and try to achieve. Diversity, the horrid spoilsport, always coming up with misunderstandings and hurt feelings. Diversity, destroyer of a team's velocity. Diversity, the Big Bad Mouse of the community, the company, the fun.

Diversity cannot go on. But what to do?

Often, the suggested solution is to limit diversity, erase it where we can – in a mood of *people like ourselves will do better together*.

And yet, if cooperative organisational frameworks of late have learned to deploy cross-functionality in teams, it is in an attempt not only to bring together team members of different skill sets, but also people of different skill-set cultures - as a power engine for sparkling exchange and smooth delivery of stories, made possible by the fireworks of relentless intercultural conversations.

Diversity is where people best learn, with, from and among each other.

For this reason, learning design should permit for a variety of skill sets and skill-set cultures to assemble and be together and perform the practice of learning.

conditions of belonging

Not if.
Not when.
Right now.
As is.
We are worthy of love and belonging.
#brenebrown

For diverse teams to be apt to learn together and add value through diversity, certain conditions must be fulfilled.

The most important of these conditions is the existence of a safe space, in which a free flow of learner's user stories can emerge, unleashing the full potential of cultural addition and multiplication.

In order to make this work, the idea of *culture* needs to be liberated from its politically defined interpretation – where culture is a artefact ascribed to territories, states, ethnic groups, power hierarchies, languages and other man-made concepts.

In order to make this work, the idea of *culture* needs to be given back to the individual, entrusted with a faculty of choice, who can at the same time subscribe to, or unsubscribe from, as many cultural frameworks as she deems appropriate – always finding threads that connect and tapestries on which to belong.

invitation

Having started from learner's user stories, the design of a learning track should hit off with structures of invitation.

Invitation should be practised towards a group of learners as diverse as possible.

Invitation is an art. You have a party in mind and you eagerly want your friends to come over and share in the fun and contribute to the celebration. Your party has no specific goal and doesn't need one: a celebration is never complete, and the joy of sharing together does never reach its final destination. There is no just-in-time.

Learning is an everlasting feast.

When was the last time you really felt invited to participate? – is the sort of Peter-Block-flavoured question I am reminded of here. [2]

When was the last time you really felt invited to participate at work?

When was the last time you really felt invited to contribute to a learning programme?

When was the last time you really felt invited to add your value to a cooperative learning space?

When was the last time you really felt invited to join and seek added, additional, hitherto undiscovered meaning, in the space, plane, volume, time and words of the working community to which you belong?

voluntary participation

True invitations imply voluntary participation. If nobody ever turns up at the parties you organize, reconsider your attempts at the art of invitation.

In the many years of my work as a facilitator of teacher training and trainer training programmes, here is one of the subjects that come up most often: that teachers and trainers and workshop facilitators are confronted with unwilling participants, who have no clue of why they are attending this or that programme or workshop, other than that their managers have told them so.

I think this issue is easy to solve. As a host who attempts perfect hospitality, I am not the one to turn a guest away, not even an unwilling one. I make it a point to rephrase an invitation – offering choice and the possibility to opt out. My invitation would be kind, gentle, friendly and reassuring.

Now that you are here, do not go away without a cup of coffee and a bite.

Now that you are here, why don't you give this a chance – for an hour or so – and please don't leave without giving me a chance to thank you for staying a while and say goodbye.

Know that you are invited to stay. I am sure we can learn so much from you. Thank you for offering us even the smallest bit of your valuable time.

In an exformative learning context, participation is driven by invitation, but remains voluntary at all times.

Exformation is a *communication method by making things unknown.* [3]

In the case of non-voluntary participation, the knowns are obligation, oppression, being small, being treated without due respect, being a prisoner of unwanted circumstances.

Transformation of these knowns into the unknowns of being together and taking part in a cooperative learning track – this transformation is the doorway towards keenness to participate, share and take a stand.

In an exformative learning space, participants embrace the unknowns of invitation. They do not need to know all the details upfront.

They just step in.

nagenda

Exformative learning design avoids gerundives, *to-be-done's*, as much as it turns away from imperatives, *you-shall-do's*.

There is no must-do and there is no must-act.

There are no *agenda* or *corrigenda*.

What must is obligatory and what must be done ("agenda") is a pre-defined list, thought up and prescribed by one who knows or pretends to do so.

Having an agenda is informative. Learning is exformative.

Informative training is agenda-driven. Exformative learning is user-driven.

Informative training is transmission of known to should-be-known, *agenda!*

Exformative learning is deconstructing what is known and exploring the unknown, *nagenda*.

purpose

This doesn't mean that there is no purpose.

The purpose of a learning track is to walk the path and walking the path is learning. Walking the path takes time – and the journey is made together, practising conversations and building relationships *en-route*.

In essence, learning paths can go anywhere from here - like toddlers will randomly stray into woodlands and fields, lost in unabated curiosity, following the trail of an insect, then seeing a bird, then frolicking with a butterfly, wondering about a flower - to finally doze off somewhere in the sand, showered by a hot afternoon sun.

For most of us, grown-ups, the sensation of being without a known destination, or even the mere suggestion of aimlessness, is upsettingly unnerving - and taking pleasure in not knowing where one is, is a joy reserved for the few.

When in doubt, when lost, it should help to know that there is indeed a purpose. Our common purpose is the journey itself.

When participation is both by invitation and voluntary, assemblies on the journey will naturally engage in liberating conversations and establishing meaningful relationships.

The journey is the learning space. The purpose is to learn.

curiosity

When it comes to exploring unknowns, young children are relentless, unstoppable, never ready-for-bed.

For adults, who so often have lost the faculty of seemingly unpurposeful inquisitiveness, exformative learning is not an easy practice. Walking the path is one, finding meaning in its steps another.

It takes an unknown amount of curiosity to be apt at exploring unknowns and leaving the safe havens of certainties and knowns behind and travel thither, boldly and unafraid.

When I was a young student at the jungle hermitage of Buduruvagala in the south-east of Sri Lanka, my teacher Obbegoda Dhammatilaka Thera kept reprimanding me with a riddle that went more or less like this:

Be curious and play, be doubtful!
Always question everything!
is what I'm sure I hear the Buddha sing.

This said – the more we grow up and get serious and replace curiosity with knowing, the harder it is for us to walk the path of exformative learning.

structures

Creativity doesn't need to be taught.
Creativity needs to be liberated.
#johncleese

Then what can we do? How to get us back into the fold of seemingly unpurposeful curiosity and youthful exploratory play and inquisitive doubt?

Perhaps the art of exploration is uncovered by the art of looking at ourselves.

To look at ourselves, we need real or imaginary objects – like a mirror, a surface of water, a sheet of polished metal, an album with photos and mementos, a smartphone in selfie mode, or perhaps a space for meditation or mental reflection.

Or a stage on which to act out a play.

Ever since its early beginnings, in Greece and China and Japan and India, theatre has been a meta-structure offering both the players and the audience an opportunity to look at, and learn about, themselves and the others.

There isn't much about it. Anyone can do theatre – even actors.

Come to think of it, all of us use theatre all of the time. We play and act and we use theatrical enactments to say things and express ideas that we couldn't say or express in any other way. From simple marriage proposals to religious rituals to recruitment interviews to parliamentary debates: it is theatrical forms that allow us to get stuff done.

To bring us back to wholesome exformative learning, to liberate our faculty of creativity and inquisitiveness, like theatre needs a stage and theatrical forms, we need wholesome structures allowing us to learn.

Structures, not for transferral of information, but allowing space for meaningful planes and shapes and time and words to emerge – and for unknowns to be explored.

Structures, allowing space in which curiosity and questioning and conversations and relationships occur. Space that holds the readiness and keenness to learn.

Space, ready for interest, value, meaning and beauty.

During the many years of my practice, with children and young adults in slums and on paddy fields, with young professionals in start-ups and multinationals, with operators in plants and farmers on fields, with activists in NGO's and educators and caregivers in schools and homes for those with special needs, with clients and patients in healthcare institutions – wherever I have worked, I have seen that without structures, exformative learning is a dead duck.

People seem to be forever in need of structures having an in-built affordance for events to unfold. It is structures that provide the medium for steps to be taken on the path. Structures are the air in which we seem to move.

Without structures, the process of exformation gets stalled, our conversations obliterated into meaningless chit-chats, practised by knowers of knowns, while our relationships remain locked in self-forged shackles of hollow superficiality.

iterations

But working with structures entails more than offering one structure after another.

Structures should be varied, each one providing a learning outcome holding value and offering affordance for a next structure to emerge.

Learning structures should be offered in sequence, one after the other, in perfect balance, at the same time mind-triggering and aesthetically pleasing, offering an uninterrupted learning value stream.

Learning structures should come in iterations – the shorter the better, for the very short provide a near continuous flow of value, forever feeding the learner's appetite for more.

reviews and retrospectives

I magine walking a hill.

Create a safe space first. Wait for a day not too cold and not too wet and not too hot and take your children with you on a hill climbing venture – like once I did on Mt. Takashiho, in the Kirishima National Park on the isle of Kyushu, Japan.

The young ones kick the pebbles and speed away and leave you behind, in your slow but steady gait.

Only till you find them beyond a curve or a bend in the path, panting on a rock, exhausted, desperate – in a state of readiness to give it all up: keenness, curiosity, drive, intent, motivation, pleasure, joy.

We sit together for a while, panting in sync, and then we laugh and look back, look down, oh wonder, what have we climbed, how high have we risen, whatever have we seen, explored, discovered.

And we chat and we enquire about how we are and how do you feel and what do you need to get on with it – and we bond and hug and share food and ready ourselves for a next lap.

A review provides rest and togetherness, while reflecting on what we have done. A retrospective reflects on how we are and what we need from each other and where do we want to go from here and are we ready to go forth.

And off we go for another dash - and after ever so much iterations of wearing out our boots and looking back and having learned about rocks and plants and butterflies and volcanic activity and sudden changes in the weather and ourselves and how strong we are and what we need to be able to do this folly thing …, we are on the hill and we stand on the edge and we shout each other's name into the wind and we wonder: however did we get up here?

*climbing Mt. Takashiho, Kirishima
Miyazaki Prefecture, Japan, July 2018*

exformative design

The quest, then, for the exformative learning designer, is difficult.
The quest, then, for the exformative learning designer, is simple.

It is to collect learner's user stories and find common areas for exploration.

Send out invitations, probing for voluntary participation by a group of individuals or a team as diverse as can be.

Offer nagenda, opening doors for a transformation of knowns into unknowns, urging relentless curiosity and sharpening the mind.

Enter the learning space.

Make it a safe and holding space.

Offer an array of learning structures, fitting into each other like tessellations, motivating and aesthetically appealing, in quick iterations, nearly a continuous flow, interspersed with reviews and retrospectives.

Get learning done. Get more learning done.

And keep learning going.

go on and on and on

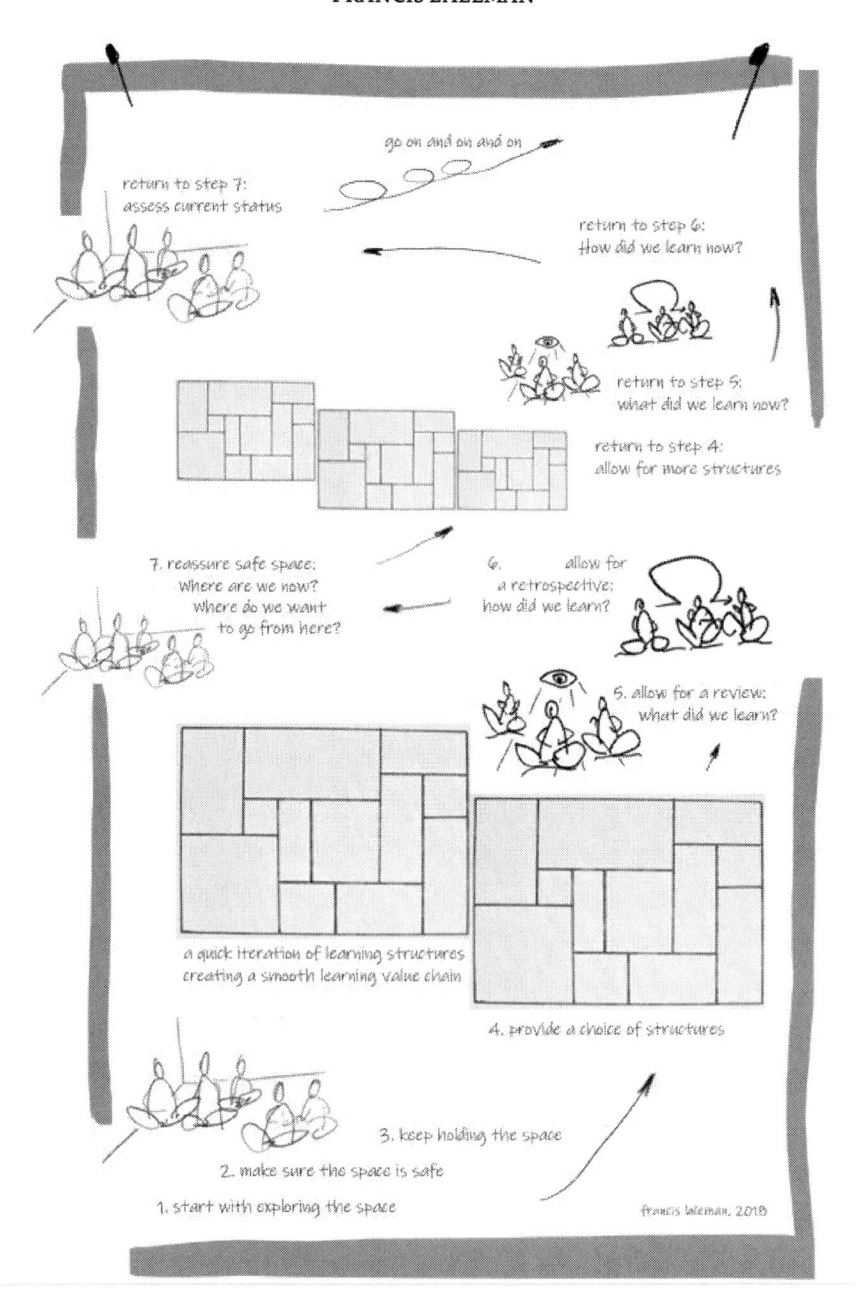

return to step 7:
assess current status

return to step 6:
How did we learn now?

return to step 5:
what did we learn now?

return to step 4:
allow for more structures

7. reassure safe space:
where are we now?
where do we want
to go from here?

6. allow for
a retrospective:
how did we learn?

5. allow for a review:
what did we learn?

a quick iteration of learning structures
creating a smooth learning value chain

4. provide a choice of structures

3. keep holding the space
2. make sure the space is safe
1. start with exploring the space

francis laleman, 2018

the exformative facilitation method

design vs facilitation

Exformative learning design is meant to provide *affordance* for exformative learning to happen, like a chair provides *affordance* to be sat upon and a stairway has the *affordance* for it to be mounted.

Likewise, exformative learning facilitation implies the creation of affordances.

An affordance is an inherent feature, present in a structure or an object or a process, allowing for the user to engage into a meaningful relationship with it. In this sense, an affordance is what a structure, object or process allows the user to do with it - without consulting a manual.

Being *in* the process, and the process not really having too much structures of its own sake, the learning process facilitator becomes as much of a designer as the designer proper.

Exformative learning is learning like a toddler: ad hoc, instantaneous and therefore always just-in-time, in iterations sometimes so brief, that time stretches out and on and over, obliterating the idea of iterations altogether, creating an uninterrupted stream of learning value increments.

This turns the exformative learning facilitator into an instant creator of affordance, allowing for learning value to materialize, very much like an agile practitioner, with a constant focus on, and working with, the items on the left of the Agile Manifesto (2001). [4]

Closely following up on the learners as human beings, and on their interactions, she proceeds, building on the value increments of learning that have occurred, always offering new structures, reflecting on how their affordance is understood and acted upon by the learners, adapting and adjusting if necessary, in close collaboration with the group before her, and instantaneously responsive to any changes that might occur along the way.

Indeed, the exformative learning facilitator is by nature at the same time an exformative designer and an agile facilitator, a gentle facilitator, a cooperative facilitator.

He is an agile facilitator, because his facilitation work happens to be an embodiment of the agile valuation system [5] – tending to see value in people and interactions rather than in processes and tools, in stuff that works rather than in comprehensive documentation, in user collaboration rather than in user negotiation, and in responsiveness to change rather than in following a plan.

She is an exformative facilitator rather than a facilitator, period – because she isn't bent on the transferral of knowns between knowers and knowers-not-yet, but rather, she offers affordance for knowns to become unknown, knowers to become knowers-not-yet, and knowers-not-yet to embrace the unknown.

If there is anything that the exformative learning facilitator knows, pun intended, it is that the transferral of knowns will only ever lead to what was already known. It is in the exploration of the unknown that new possibilities emerge.

gentle facilitation

In order for a facilitator to be able to offer allowances on the fly, and nothing much more than that, she needs to be a gentle cooperative facilitator.

A gentle person is someone having or showing a mild, kind, or tender temperament or character. Similar concepts are: being benign, humane, lenient, considerate, understanding, compassionate, sweet-tempered.

Gentle facilitators are moderate in action and effect. They are the opposite of strong or violent.

Gentle facilitation is not an easy piece of art. It requires the skills of both being there and not being there, intent observation, instantaneous artistry with structures, deep level knowledge of affordances and what they allow the user to do, wilful non-intervention, affordance-driven intervention, systemic sensitivity, staying tuned with many individuals at the same time, understanding group phenomena, and many more.

In gentle facilitation, all of us are students.

being there or not

Many times I have asked my facilitator students to stand or sit, grounded on the floor, and draw or paint an imaginary circle around them, shielding them from all outside influences - and close their eyes and think and think twice and think some more and remain standing or seated until they know who they are, who they really are – only to leave them puzzled and unnerved and sometimes disturbed, either because they didn't understand the assignment - or perhaps because they did.

And yet, this is exactly the exformative facilitator's position. Of being there or not being there, of how it doesn't matter whether one is there or one is not, because the very question whether one is there or one is not, implies a subject, an ego, and it is this subject that we cannot find.

Unless I thrive on the illusion that

I know
and thou knowest not,

there is no *I* without *the other*.

systemic unity

Subject and object are one. A human being's existence, in its very essence, assumes the existence of other beings – and since my existence assumes yours, it is in the relationship we have with one another that we co-create one another's existence.

I am reminded here, of a key premise in Adlerian psychology: If all interpersonal relationships were to disappear from our world, we, human beings, would cease to exist as we exist now. There would no longer be affordance for togetherness, exchange, or learning. Information would become futile – and exformation would hardly fare better. [6]

The gentle facilitator exists but in systemic unity with what defines her: the space and the people therein, and the activities taking place and the relationships being shaped and being developed and being fostered.

The gentle facilitator is a practitioner who doesn't practise, because outside his practice he is nought.

All of us humans are continuously being shaped and moulded by what we do in an ever changing environment, by the relationships we have within that environment, and by the phenomenon of continuous change thereof.

Exformative learning is a process of learning, a process that never stops, allowing for continuous transformation, so smoothly iterative that there is no time for a subject to ever *be*, wandering as he ever is in the realms of *becoming*.

And the hardest thing for a facilitator is to allow for that becoming, herself included.

RESOURCEFUL EXFORMATION

adlerian perspective
Arken Museum for Modern Art, Copenhagen, July 2019

intent observation

In order to keep becoming rather than being content with being, and in order to invite others to keep becoming rather than being content with being, one needs a high level of awareness.

The awareness required of the exformative learning facilitator should make it possible for her to guard over the uninterrupted flow of a learning value stream – constantly generating affordances for becoming, for letting go of the known and veering off into the realms of the unknown.

Exformation was defined by Kenia Hara, a designer by profession, as *a communication method by making things unknown* – a method which is easier to design than to practise, because in our case not only does the designer design, but so does the facilitator and, ultimately, every member of the exformative learning group.

Designing affordances is one thing, designing affordances that really allow for users to act upon what is afforded, is another.

Intent observation, then, is the faculty possessed by the facilitator, of continuously tuning in, reading into every detail of the present systemic (im)balance, always being on guard, nimbly filling up every occurring affordance, in order for herself and the group to be able to embed yet new affordance, allowing for co-creation of new learning value increments, driving the process on and on.

seeing more than the obvious

What do you see? – I would ask my students, while I make them look at a segment of purely white wall.

I see a white wall, one says, with not a small dose of complacency.

I see nothing at all, there is nothing at all, sighs another, with a bit of despair.

The artist sees a landscape of possibilities, an open plane, ready to accept shapes and colours and incorporating endless place for excitement and adventure.

The facilitator sees a wall. Slightly shaded towards the left end, suggesting an ever-so-slight curvature, quite invisible if it weren't for the somewhat darker end. With a hint of far-off sunlight, travelling ever-so-slowly from one side to another. A plane in plaster, violently out-of-white. The colour, rather, of humidity, in the lightest shade of grey, not quite the white of the shell of an egg, yet with a hint of the same texture, in there, a smoothness that invites the act of stroking it with the palm of one's hand. And yet, a violent wall, and graceful in the act, withholding its affordance for near full-out reflection of light, just enough to allow for the beholder to be confronted by it.

What do you see? – I would ask my students, while I make them look at a group of workshop participants in the process of having a conversation.

I see them talking, one says, with not a small dose of complacency.

I see five of them in a group, there is nothing much more to see, sighs another, with a bit of despair.

The artist sees a narrative, a story. She sees how the group is perfectly positioned between the wall and the window, in a perpendicular beam of morning light. She draws a frame. They are discussing something, what could it be? With two of them sitting down writing and three of them standing behind, it looks like a moment of historic importance. The signing of a peace treaty? The acquisition of a house? A business? What is possible? Where can this go?

The facilitator sees a structure, a fragment of systemic connections. Five people. Two of them sitting, writing, three standing. Are they together? Are they involved? Are they learning? Have they stepped into the structure offered, have they subtly shifted? Adjusted? Are they in sync with the others present in the room? Is there a sense of lasting inquisitiveness? Is there drive? Is the current distribution of people in the room effective, at all? Is the current constellation pregnant of more to come? Where in this moment, in this constellation, is the affordance for what to do next?

RESOURCEFUL EXFORMATION

intent observation of whiteness
Bayt al-Andalus, Antwerp, December 2017

facilitation as art

Clearly, then, it is in observation of the space of *when and where does affordance emerge for what to do next*, that art and exformative facilitation hold hands.

From art, I have learned that the presence of people, an *audience* if you want, is not a mere accident but verily a *raison d'être* of what it is I am doing. [7]

From art I take that time is needed for transformation, of the individual, myself and the other, of the social construct, the team, the community, the organisation.

From art I take that creativity is not the goal but a medium, allowing for stories to emerge.

That utopia is an accessible realm of reality.

That everybody wants to be understood, that everybody wants to understand.

Just like is the case in experiential art, exformative facilitation continuously suggests affordance for voluntary participation – not necessarily of the kind that is perceived as meaningful as from the very first moment, but always of the sort that becomes meaningful through interactions and conversations, and treading forward in the medium of time.

Just like in art, the participation sought after by the exformative facilitator is sometimes an act of play, with confusion as a temporary companion, inoffensive and unfeared, on grounds of its sweet and fragrant language, gently hinting at possibilities, opportunities and easy affordance for smiling acceptance and embrace of a unexpected misstep here and some uneasiness or faltering there.

Just like art, education and learning are not about the transmission of knowns and fragments of consensus - rather, like an artist, the exformative learning facilitator prepares affordance for knowns and consensus to get disrupted, to get unchained, exformed and redirected, towards an embrace of unknowns and possibilities for change and growth and evolution.

Like an artist, the exformative learning facilitator holds a space where there is no room for established truths that belong to the realms of status quo, an intrusive beast, always on the lookout to pin us down in *what was* and *what already is*.

Like an artist, the exformative learning facilitator creates a forum that allows for new meanings to emerge, a gentle breeze, lifting us up from *what was* and *what already is* into the realms of *what can be* and *what can also be* and *what could be* and *what else could be if only*.

Neither art nor education or learning has to do with convincing people to think or do anything in particular.

Both are offers of voluntary participation, into a process where exploration and conversations take place, through which possibilities and opportunities for new insights are explored and sometimes discovered.

Neither art nor education or learning exists on its own. Neither demands, but both provide an offer for a common ground of understanding, a common world of reference that makes the artist, *in casu* the exformative learning facilitator and the learner or workshop participant, fundamentally equal.

the real value

La valeur réelle de l'art est en fonction de son pouvoir de révélation libératrice, said René Magritte, famously.

La valeur réelle de la facilitation exformative est en fonction de son pouvoir de révélation libératrice, I reply.

RESOURCEFUL EXFORMATION

la valeur réelle
dialogues with Blacka Di Danca
Antwerp, November 2019

conversation and imagination

Indeed, even if the artist creates on her very own, in his very private world or body or mind, and even if one could hold the view that art is very much an individual expression of a most individual state of imagination, there is no art as such without an intent of expression – and an expression being a conversational device, there can be no art without a beholder, a person or persona with whom to entertain a conversation.

So art is conversation? – Perhaps more than that.

If I paint or dance or read you the haiku of the day – my idea might not just be to express myself or engage in conversation – I might be offering you a vehicle, for you to ride, having embedded the affordance for a journey of imagination.

The journey of *your* imagination.

Seen in this way, my art is a facilitator's device – an artefact, born out of purpose, allowing expression and inviting participation and action – none of which are pre-defined or have a detailed list of requirements – all of which are open, throbbing with the expectation of something as yet unexplored and hitherto unknown.

Nothing is fixed upfront. As Bruce Mau and Rem Koolhaas, of OMA fame, have suggested in 1995 [8], whenever a journey of imagination is at play, we can either lean back and observe and watch in wonder and document our overwhelming awe for what is, or we can laugh the professional field as it exists out of existence and dismantle it and re-create a field of imagination-grown reality, holding affordance for exformation and wonder.

The point is that both are possible reactions to art and both are activities of learning - and neither can exist unless there is a process of conversation with others.

cooperative facilitation

Therefore, by the mere fact that exformation and exformative learning, and exformative learning facilitation, all exist in the realms of both art and imagination, exformation is by definition an intently cooperative process.

The exformative learning facilitator is not a facilitator *per se*, she is a facilitator of shared, cooperative facilitation.

In this sense, the act of exformative facilitation is nothing more than being a placeholder on which mutual and cooperative facilitation can emerge and exist.

How to explain this?

It was during an intercultural Gentle Cooperative Facilitation workshop in the early summer of 2017 that I first thought of using a videotape of Cut Piece by Yoko Ono to illustrate the idea.

Cut Piece, first performed in 1964 at the Yamaichi Concert Hall in Kyoto, is a shocking piece to say the least, with the performance artist seated on stage allowing members of the audience to come towards her, one by one, and cut away a piece of her clothing.

And cut away, the members of the audience do indeed - piece by piece of first her clothes and then her underwear disappearing, while step by step her nudity is revealed. In due time she is utterly naked, humiliated, reviled, objectified, denuded of the bare essence of her humanity.

Meanwhile, everyone in the room has turned from onlooker to participant to actor, everyone is co-responsible, everyone is in it. The artist herself merely has offered a placeholder on which events have the possibility to unfurl. The real facilitators, of the ultimate conversation and ensuing lessons on morality and ethics, are in the audience.

Wait, they are not *in* the audience, they *are* the audience.

Among the participants, some literally *do* something, going to the stage and cutting away a piece of Yoko's garments. But others, by doing nothing at all, do as much, or more. They perform the act of doing nothing, facilitating the ensuing conversation just as much as everyone else.

In the end, a considerable piece of learning value increment is delivered, open and pregnant with further possibilities, having been co-facilitated by a set of actors, non-actors in fact, who have trodden the plane, invited thereto, but by all means voluntarily, in a space offered by the exformative facilitator herself, featuring enough affordance for the attendants-turned-facilitators to act, the lessons to emerge and the learning value increment to substantiate.

Thus, cooperative facilitation is the facilitation of a cooperative facilitation effort. By virtue of presenting a structure featuring affordance, attendants step in and become facilitators themselves, facilitating each other, with and among each other, co-creating the learning process in real time.

RESOURCEFUL EXFORMATION

interacting with Cut Piece
42 Acres, Shoreditch, London, June 2019

exformative facilitation

In brief, exformative facilitation is gentle, instantaneous and artful facilitation, practised by a facilitator with the intent of meaningful observation, both present and unpresent, suggesting structures with in-built affordance for co-operative facilitation of emergent conversations by a group of participants-turned-actors, learning with, from and among each other.

In this, the idea of exformative learning facilitation coincides with the mutual approach to learning and education suggested by Paulo Freire in 1968 [9] – an educational framework for the co-creation of knowledge, skilful knowledge and knowledgeable skills, which Freire promised to be fully authentic, from and by the people - and allowing individuals and teams to practise interactions and conversations generating awareness of their (as yet) incompleteness - and to look forward to becoming more resourceful and more fully human.

Learning and personal development are both an unalienable individual right and an act of unconditional engagement of the individual towards the team, the organisation, the community.

Through exformation, L&D, Learning & Development, is being freed from its top-bottom imperatives and being returned to the grassroots where it belongs.

Like Freire's proposal, exformative learning facilitation is an attempt to use learning and education as a means of consciously returning resourcefulness to individuals and teams in order for them to have the means to shape their own skillsets, and attribute value and meaning to the spaces, planes, volumes, time and words of their own environment, their own organisations.

With all this, exformative learning facilitation is a practice of *conscientization* pur sang.

RESOURCEFUL EXFORMATION

stepping up, speaking out
JES dance battle, Antwerp, November 2017

exformative structures

facilitation with structures

Would it be possible, by bluntly disregarding the cycle of exchanging already-known information, the I-know-cycle, to create a learning framework that would act as an entrance for curiosity? Is communication possible which, rather than making the world known, makes people understand how little they know of the world?

My questions are the same as Kenya Hara's [10] – and with him, I suggest that

*if you can figure out how much you don't know,
the method by which you will know it will appear naturally.*

Having established that exformative learning facilitation is very much like art, and only existing in dialogue with its environment and the people therein - it won't come as a surprise that exformative learning facilitation requires placeholders, a canvas, a stage or a dancefloor or anything, structures in brief - providing a medium through which learning conversations, the objects of the very facilitation practice, can emerge.

structures of play

*T**he world is a playground:*
without end, the play of life
is being enacted before me,

wrote Ghalib, the famous Urdu poet, sometime in the early nineteenth century. [11]

Play is older than culture, went on Johan Huizinga a century later, for culture, however inadequately defined, always presupposes human society - and animals have not waited for man to teach them their playing. [12]

In esssence, play is free, and when engaged upon by the free, play represents freedom.

It is, perhaps, in loving memory of the freedom experienced by the as yet unfettered player, that by the unfree, play is sensed to have such liberating force.

The liberating power of play is strongly interconnected with its exformative process. Lest being predictive and dull and uninviting, play is always engaging towards the unknown and creating unexplored outcomes.

Play is also a placeholder, essentially different from real life, perhaps even unconnected to it. Play is whatever is not ordinary, it is a canvas on which we co-create possibilities and imaginary events, within the temporarily offered constraints of space and plane and volume and time and word.

Play is exploratory. It urges the player to touch and smell and feel and embody all corners of what could be and what could also be.

Being a placeholder for exformative exploration, play also exists on the plane or playground of the mind, in a space of its own, which the mind creates for it.

Play, therefore, is poiesis, poetry, as well as mythopoiesis, myth-making – both of them functionalities laying otherwise dormant in the informative sphere.

In fact, not just play is a canvas for poetry and myth - the same is true of the bond between play and music and dance and the other arts – all forever balancing on a rope stretching from the formalities and disciplines of the known, the status-quo, towards the other shore, where exformation waits with a welcoming smile, luring the acrobat into the realms of newer meanings, other values, parallel possibilities and the attractions of as yet unknown destinations.

Surely, structures of play are as essential to learning as they are to art?

We needn't look far to get the idea. When learning games are being played, Augusto Boal's Games for Actors and Non-Actors, 1992, a true classic in its genre, is never far away from sight – and neither is the exceptional output of the living legend Sivasailam Thiagarajan [13], aka Thiagi, who, with Boal, has elevated the concept of play to its rightful place, centerstage in the process of education and growth and the acquisition of resourcefulness in human beings.

natural learning

I keep wishing for everyone to have become familiar with the concept of free play early in life, always feeling deep personal pain and a strong sense of loss whenever I come across workshop participants who haven't.

In the course of my early field work in India I have had the good luck to see quite a bit of play in action, not in regular schools or corporate education, but in rural villages and slums, and in grassroots educational projects based on the philosophies and educational approaches taken by the likes of Augusto Boal - but also Maria Montessori, and, more so, Rabindranath Tagore. [14]

This helped me experiment with game-based learning structures early on in my own learning facilitation story - and the formative influence of these trials (and errors) on my later work can hardly be overestimated.

Tagore, for one, believed that we should do everything in our power to recognize how for the young child, learning through exformation comes as a natural, spontaneous, and organic capability. As learning facilitators, it should be our priority to protect the student from the loss of this faculty - a painful seperation, generally initiated by the world of grown-ups and its focus on the transmission of information, from as early as the age of thirty-or-so months.

Gurudev, as Tagore was both affectionately and reverently known, passed away in 1941 and the very word *exformation* had not been coined at the time. Therefore, during the more than half a century of his life as a poet, composer, choreographer, painter, playwright, philosopher and educationalist, he consistently spoke *of natural learning* – but it is chrystal clear that what he meant is exactly the same stuff.

Learning, for the young child, is essentially explorative, active and full of joy. The challenge of education, then, is to enable a continuation of this natural way of learning - always paving the way for the widest possible development of an individual's interests.

It all sounds familiar by now: The means to do this, suggests Tagore, are contained in the learning facilitator's provision of educational structures focused on the continuous development and growth of human feelings, emotions, self-reliance and communal cooperation – using any of the arts as a medium.

Have you found Teirlinck's division of space, plane, volume, time and word somewhat vague? A tad artificial? – Tagore would be at your side.

The arts and their carriers of creative expression are one and the same, he pertains. They are a continuum of concepts and structures, reflecting the world but clearly separate from it, apart enough to provide the safety and freedom of play, and make room for boundless exploration of the realms of impermanence, uncertainties and change.

And more: the arts are the gift of the young.

By excellence, the arts are the structures of play in which the young engage, driven by an entirely natural keenness, completely free of informational thought.

Information belongs to the world of subject-based knowledge transmission. With natural learning and exformative learning as a guideline, learning proper can no longer exist as a subject-centred construct - for subjects are vessels, containing no more than constrained information.

Exformation means activity-and-relationship-centred learning, which unleashes creativity, a sense of wonder, and a keenness to explore the unknown.

retrospection as a structure of play
JES dance battle, Antwerp, November 2019

structures of liberation

Keeping Tagore's concept of natural learning in mind, and not forgetting Huizinga's suggestion that play is essentially a structure played by the free, the exformative learning facilitator might struggle to use play in an environment of being locked into information and inaccessibility of imagination.

For most facilitators, having to work in such an environment is a daily reality – and for this reason, the need to address this difficulty is substantial.

Turning around situations featuring lack of invitation and absence of voluntary participation, is difficult enough. The participants are prisoners of the system. They are where they don't want to be – and, as Paulo Freire would have said, they are treated as empty bank accounts, waiting to get stuffed with information they do not want or need, but is sure to bring return to the investor. [15]

What is it, then, that the exformative learning facilitator can do?

She can only turn to offering appropriate structures, at first sight adding constraints to the systemic whole, perhaps causing a perception of even more oppression.

And yet, exformative practice shows that structures of constraint, if neatly designed and well applied, are the shortest route to the experience of liberation.

Imagine playing a game of sorts, say shogi or chess. You are being restrained to a small, two-dimensional plane, on which the game will unfold. You are being subjected to a condense but demanding set of rules. You are being submitted to an array of play conditions, trust between the players being not the least of them – while you are being imprisoned by the imposed conditions' uncertainty.

Truly, the game of shogi, or chess, is a structure of enormous constraint. And look, it takes a player for us to provide testimony of how the constraints of the game are in fact enablers of the freedom experienced in playing the game.

The idea of this ebullient liberation (of the mind) was masterfully put into words by Dhanpat Rai Shrivastava, aka Munshi Premchand (1880-1936), a contemporary of Rabindranath Tagore's, in a story called The Chess Players[16] – in 1977 brought to the screen by Satyajit Ray, with an unforgettable Amjad Khan in the role of Wajid Ali Shah, King of Awadh, and Richard Attenborough impersonating General James Outram, the king's nemesis.

Or think of Tagore's own story of liberation through constraint – as told in Dak Ghar, The Post Office, a true wonder of a little book, written in the course of no more than four days in 1912.[17]

In Dak Ghar, Amal is a weak little boy, for reasons of health restrained to the confines of just one room, with a single window giving way to the courtyard of a house. Through this window, the boy talks to passers-by, asking them endless questions about life outside, and in particular about the places people go. The construction of a new post office opposite the house prompts the imaginative Amal to fantasize about one day receiving a letter from the king. The village headman, having decided to go along with Amal's wishful thinking, pretends the child has indeed received a letter from the king, promising that the royal physician will come to the village and attend to the boy and make him better.

For good reasons, Dak Ghar became an instant hit. Amal is perceived as the ultimate personification of liberation through constraint – while his natural zest for inquisitiveness, curiosity, imagination and wonder have become the standard outcome desired by what Tagore called *natural learning* - and what we are now considering as *learning through exformation*.

After openings in London and Kolkata, The Post Office successfully ran in interwar Germany. It was translated into the French by André Gide and read out on national radio the night before Paris fell to the Nazis. A Polish version was performed in the Warsaw ghetto, under the supervision of the reputed educator, author, pedagogue and social activist Henryk Goldszmit, aka Janusz Korczak (1878-1942), who would perish in the Treblinka extermination camp not more than a month-or-so later.

The extraordinary power of The Post Office as a structure of liberation, or a metaphor thereof, has been noticed by a series of stage directors, actors and educationalists ever since. In India, the play was taken up in the 2010s by Heisnam Kanhailal, the legendary founder of Kalakshetra Manipur, a theatre laboratory established in 1969, with the aim of exploring new vocabularies for the existing language of drama and performance – somewhat in the footsteps of Jerzy Grotowski's concept of *poor theatre*.

It was a coincidence that both Arka Mukhopadhyay, poet, performer and director at his Theatre of Resonance, and I, were working on the same Tagore material when we started our conversations in the spring of 2018.

This coincidence brought about a most wonderful exchange, that would lead to Arka's major grassroots educational project *In Search of Amal* in India, and my *Amal: Working with the Child Within* workshops at HRD Academy in Belgium.

RESOURCEFUL EXFORMATION

waiting for the king's letter
Europawijk, Geel, Belgium, October 2019

exformation: opening the king's letter

Like Tagore's introduction of an imaginary post office, the structures deployed by an exformative learning facilitator should be artfully and appropriately designed, showing adequate affordance for the student to break through the confines embedded in the structure's formal circumscription - and experience a exhilirating sense of liberation.

When learning is merely a transmission of information, the recipient of information keeps receiving the king's letters – but all of them remain unopened and none of the possibilities contained in them shall ever see the light.

When learning is a practice of exformation, the post office becomes a gateway for letters to arrive, envelopes to be opened and stories to emerge.

liberating structures

On a somewhat lighter footing, or perhaps better phrased for today's corporate audience, in 2014, Henri Lipmanowicz and Keith McCandless have come up with what they have labelled *liberating structures* – suggesting a powerful antidote to the informative ways of learning that have been dominating corporate life for all too long. [18]

Devised as an answer to the conventional, purely informational structures commonly applied in corporate environments, think of PowerPoint presentations, status reports and managed discussions – *liberating structures* call for people to use light-weight, non-pptx-based formats, uniquely adapted to mutual exchange, cooperative work and co-creation.

What follows, then, is a delightful series of 30+ structures, mostly conversational and sometimes genuinely exformative, even if perhaps not always aesthetically appealing.

In a matter of just a few years, the Lipmanowicz and McCandless liberating structures have acquired cult status, mostly with the young and not the least in circles of Scrum Masters and assorted agilists – growing fast into what is now a sweeping Liberating Structures Movement, complete with its own master practitioners and superfacilitators.

The LS community thrives on global membership and an open-source growing list of structures – making it great fun and providing an excellent base from which exformative practice can penetrate the world of work.

And more: many of the liberating structures can be used in a learning & development context – providing an appealing opportunity to combine adoption of interactivity, play and cooperative learning, with a novel approach to organisational learning and the emergence, perhaps, of a genuine learning organisation.

lighting up
Rasheed Raya teaching liberating structures
Bayt al-Andalus, Antwerp, June 2018

senses of embodiment

Quite different ways are explored through structures of embodiment and multisensorial learning.

In the body's constant battle with its environment and the world, the more we grow up and evolve into adulthood and old age, the more our senses seem to suffer. Brainwork gradually takes over, making us forget about our nature-given sensorial and spatial observation skills.

With time, we seem to lose the capacity to feel what we touch, listen to what we hear and see what we look at.

Equally, we can or dare no longer touch in order to feel, we listen but do no longer hear, we look but do no longer see.

Education, and conventional classes more so, have urged us into a process of digesting information, boxing-in what we know, prompting our senses to feel, listen and see no further than the knowledge horizon of our being well-informed.

"Boxing-in." It means that informational learning has crippled us into smaller size – as the body adapts itself to the job it has to do.

This is a sad affair. Adaptation of our senses into smaller sizes really feels like a loss, an irreversible turn towards limitation, the exact opposite of the idea of development and growth which are the object of our story.

For us, people, the process of adaptation should make us broader, richer, more experienced, more able to see connections and sense connectivity.

Is was Augusto Boal [19] who taught that for people, adaptation brought forth by specialization is both atrophy and hypertrophy – a chronic condition of misalignment, calling out for a cure where the body can restore itself and become able again.

A cure, a retreat, a program of reharmonization.

Reharmonizers. The word is Boal's.

Reharmonizers are structures providing affordance for learners to reconnect with multisensorial understanding of themselves and of their environment. Typically, they source energy, understanding, comprehension, yes, learning, from features of the body, our eyes, ears, hands, feet, capacity of resonance, and more – re-awakening our senses and physical responses.

I have worked with structures of embodiment in all sorts of learning environments and all kinds of learning subjects, from software to hardware, from gardening to understanding history and exercising grammar. Triggering learning by proposing a liberating structure with affordance for embodiment, comes down to identifying and finding appropriate sensorial reflexes and experiences - think of mental and physical Post-it notes, that the mind can connect to certain stages in the discovery of new meaning and new value.

Think, for example, of a senior citizen, who, even after decades of travelling through life, will always remember the particular smell emitted from the pages of her medium school maths textbook, on the very moment that she discovered the correct formula to calculate the number of matchsticks needed for the n-th surround shape triangle, given that if n=1, the number is 3.

being Amal, aka working at the post office
senses of embodiment workshop at HRD Academy, Belgium, March 2019

structures of space

Sensorial reharmonization being the main attraction of the exformative learning facilitator's destination, and senses being the turnstiles connecting the individual with her spatial environment, it is in space that the most essential of reharmonizing structures will unfold.

Space is the medium into which we are born, the borderless box that we invade as we go, and help shape and make ours as we learn and grow.

Structures of space make use of the momentum provided by an expanse when it lingers in limbo, as yet unentered, as yet undefined.

The space in which we bring people together, invited and voluntary, is an active agent in the exformative learning process. The main challenge is for the exformative learning facilitator to come up with relevant structures allowing for the territory to be explored without it being hardhandedly invaded or self-assuredly defined.

I love it when workshop participants set out to explore the workshop space using *gentle intrusion*. I insist for learners to take of their shoes before entering the room, and tread softly, like monks or nuns in a Zen monastery, as if in pursuit of perpetual wu-wei, the art of leaving no traces – and, with eyes slightly averted, take note of the arena surrounding them, almost with awe and deference, as if the sanctity of the learning space is such, that even the slightest act of invasion would defile it.

And then, when the room is truly inhabited, we profess the activity of intent observation, not looking at, but really seeing the conceptual whiteness surrounding us, and as soon as the whiteness is seen, observing it with purpose and intent.

What is the impact of space? - I like to think of what happened to me on the island of Naoshima, in Seto Naikai, the Seto Inland Sea in Japan.

In 2003, philanthropist Soichiro Fukutake commissioned the architect Tadao Ando to construct the Chichu Art Museum, on a coastal stretch of the island, as a site rethinking the relationship between nature and people. In line with the the holistic philosophies of Fukutake and his own sense of dimensions and harmony, Tadao Ando built the museum almost entirely underground (chichū) - thus avoiding the natural Seto Naikai scenery to be spoiled by man-made constructs.

The collection that the museum was meant to put on permanent display, was kept small on purpose: no more than five paintings by Claude Monet, three mesmerizing light installations by James Turrell, and a grand piece of *meaningless work* (sic) by Walter De Maria.

Knowing all this, nothing, really nothing prepares the visitor for the experiences awaiting her on entry. Despite being nearly completely subterranean, the museum's architecture lets in an abundance of natural light, constantly altering the appearance of the artworks and the ambience of the space with the passage of time, pushing forever new shapes of *hokusai waves* of electrons through days and nights and seasons.

It is with trepidation that one wanders through a garden that could have been conceived by Monet himself, before entering the underground maze of corridors with walls of polished concrete, while softly quivering beams of daylight, emitted by largely unobserved sources, lead the way into the buried sanctuary.

Deep inside the belly of the hill, after a sensuous journey during which the visitor has lost every sense of direction and time, one at last reaches the spatial ideas around which the museum is laid out.

The Walter de Maria art space has very much the feel of a *baoli*, a stepped well – with, instead of water at the bottom, a gigantic sphere and a series of twenty-seven gilded wooden geometric forms along the steps, experienced under natural light coming in from the ceiling, continuously metamorphosizing as the world turns around its axis while the visitor stands by.

Of James Turrell, one is taken first by a window structure and a skylight, and then, overwhelmingly, by a *ganzfeld* – which is the German word to describe a phenomenon of total loss of depth perception, very much like in the experience of a white-out, but then in colour of constantly changing hue, from pink into purple into blue, and back and forth and back. Utterly losing sense of what and when and where, one does not dare to tread, lest one would fall off the sphere on which, in which, one exists – and one forgets to breathe in anticipation of a final event, some kind of conclusive *deus ex-machina*, which keeps being postponed.

Finally having pulled oneself off and out of the trance of being enveloped in Turrell's ganzfeld, one enters the shrine proper, the *cella,* the *honden,* the *garbagriha,* a *sanctum sanctorum* of absolute, indistinguishable whiteness – only interrupted by five monumental Claude Monet blues.

One is not permitted to wear shoes or to touch the paintings, but for all that is left, the experience of the room is utterly and completely the visitor's. One lingers, tries in vain to ready the body and mind for the spectacle. People sit. Some lie down, unashamedly, on the white, softly tiled, cool but welcoming floor. There is a strong sense of being weightless inside a colourless cubicle, where one doesn't know where, if anywhere at all, the floor ends and the walls begin – and one is captured by nobody and nothing else but oneself and a strangely intimate togetherness with the others in the room – all together in dialogue with Claude Monet, co-creating something new, across time and distance, an altogether new construct of whites and blues and walls and ceilings and light and shadows and motion and everlasting bliss.

RESOURCEFUL EXFORMATION

play of white, conversations with Monet
Chichu Art Museum, Naoshima, Japan, August 2018

constellations

I have never understood how constellation work, that particular structure of bringing people together in space and generating affordance for revealing play and replay in systemic connectivity, is so often practised without letting the space itself, that ultimate agent of systemic unity, play out its full potential.

Like sociometry and sociodrama, which I will discuss later, constellations derive from psychodynamic psychotherapy: they have entered the world of organisational learning only recently - and while they have steadily earned endearment by learning & development professionals, they are still taken with suspicion and hesitation by many in the corporate field. [20] [21]

Hesitation with *Aufstellungen,* aka constellations, is not always inappropriate: as a therapeutic approach, the method has been described, by scientists and therapists alike, as a form of *quantum quackery* - while even Bert Hellinger, who made the *Austellungsmethode* famous, used the widely debunked concept of so-called *morphic resonance* to explain it.

And yet, it would be sad to dismiss the method altogether – for constellations as such, when disrobed of their super-healer claim, are just another group of systemic structures in space, uniquely well adapted to being a resource for the exformative learning practitioner.

But take care, the concept is easier described than exercised.

A group of people is assembled in a convenient space and a series of affordances is being explored, in order for the group to find ways to systemically interconnect. Once this interconnection is established, a case is being put forward, most frequently by one of the participants. The facilitator than assists the holder of the case in developing the case story in space. The case holder chooses other participants to come forward, by invitation and based on voluntary participation, and embody certain persons, personae or aspects of the case. The case holder, sometimes assisted by the facilitator, further facilitates the process, moving the *representatives* (enactors) to different positions, like a contestant would do in a live shogi performance, all the time exploring affordances for less or more systemic friction or connection. Emerging insights, which is what the structure is all about, are usually discovered by the case owner, or volunteered by the enactors, based on empathy and their experiences of interconnectedness in the field.

Exformation is where the learners themselves become facilitators and are cooperatively responsible for venturing into the unknown and extracting new meaning and fresh value from this process.

Replace *case* by *user story* and *emerging insights* by *learning value increments* – and it will easily be seen that constellation work is an exformative learning structure by excellence.

In fact, *constellations* is cooperatively facilitated exformation in space.

constellation work in an art installation by Anthony McCall
LAM, Lille, France, December 2018

planar structures

While space remains of importance throughout the exformative learning process, some of the structures I use seem to exist rather on a two-dimensional plane – taking up the role of a placeholder, for the exformative learning facilitator to be enriched with built-in affordances for cooperative stories to emerge and be told and exchanged.

This can be a sheet of white paper or canvas with an affordance of being smothered with paint, invading its reflective power, urging it to leave its chrysalis of impermeability, setting it free, prodding it into absorption and refraction and meaning.

Or a piece of floor, by the facilitator's creative power transformed into the stage of a floor game, where objects and workshop participants will play out a story-related choreography and engage into dialogues and conversations.

Visual facilitation, with markers on paper, has become a recent fad, and the concept of outsider art, where *everybody can draw*, is rapidly gaining enthusiasm – but I prefer working with canvas rather than paper or cardboard, and soft pastels and acrylic paint rather than sharpies.

Working with paint provides an incomparable multisensorial extravaganza. Unscrewing the cap of a tube of paint, seeing how the dough of a pigment spaghetti is waiting in there, in the caverns of its receptacle, impatient to pop out and see the light of day – white light, by the gentle balance of absorption and refraction and reflection of which it will take the form of its true, coloured self. The indescribable excitement coming with the ASMR of the paint squirting out, driven thither by the gentle squeeze of thumb and index finger, the inexplicably satisfying *plurp* sound, with sometimes a *put!-put!*, when the splotch of paint frees itself from the tube and hops up into the air, before landing with a *plop* on the painter's palette, or wood board, or canvas...

I have never met anybody able to remain insensitive to it all.

And further, the *mixing-switching*, the *muxing* and *wuxing* of new colours, *your* colours, entirely personal, as unique as one in the billions and billions of possibilities lying open in front of you.

Surface and paint are uniquely powerful placehoders for the learner's thoughts and feelings and expressions of the moment. They are exformative because they are not trying to steer anyone in a particular, pre-digested and pre-arranged direction. Rather, they are absolutely unique, once-in-a-universe-and-time constellations of multisensoriality and pigments and light, opening up stories altogether unheard of and ready to be engulfed by meaning and value never encountered before.

Typically, the exformative learning facilitator will ask workshop participants to paint anything at all, from emotions and mindsets to customer service complaint handling scripts or parts of a distillation process.

With a set of paint works or drawings, having been made available by the participants, the facilitator will invite all to take, and come to *own*, any drawing other then their own – and share stories with the group, based on the painting of their choice, explaining perhaps why this piece of art is of their own making (while everybody knows it is not), or explaining why it couldn't be (while nobody but the artist herself knows whose painting is actually being discussed).

But it needn't be paint proper. Planar structures are uniquely suitable even for the digital classroom – where screens of mobiles and monitors, for reasons of their sheer two-dimensionality, can act in a very similar way to canvas and acryl – leaving it to the exformative learning designer to find ASMR alternatives for the scintillations and squeaks and swooshes of tubes and paint and paper or canvas.

*splotch! – an outsider art workshop
for trainers and facilitators
Bayt al-Andalus, Antwerp, Belgium, November 2019*

universal constructivism

With visual facilitation having re-surfaced in the wake of the run to dispowerpoint organisational learning, a number of visual facilitation schools have emerged, teaching students, educators, trainers and assorted facilitators a recognizable, standardized visual language – with a set grammar and a codified vocabulary of pre-coined icons.

We must be careful with this – for even if the message seems to be to propagate the baseline of outsider art, that *everybody can draw*, if the visual language in which we draw is pre-formatted by commerce-driven visual language companies, we are boxing rather than unboxing means of free creative expression – and might end up creating a visual communication field no different from the powerpoint stick figures of old – only, this time, given shape with sharpies rather than a keyboard.

Of course, the idea of creating and using a universal visual language is not new. In essence, the whole enterprise started with oracle bones in China, hieroglyphs in Egypt, old Mesoamerican writing systems and more. In fact, one could argue that for a writing system or script to be of value and serve its purpose, codification and universalism are its very conditions.

As a structure for exformative learning, however, the visual language we are after is not a fully codified one in principle – and not a universal one per se.

The work of the Uruguayan artist and toy manufacturer Joaquín Torres-Garcia (1874-1949), who was instrumental to an art movement called *Universal Constructivism*, can help us learn what I mean.

Let the practitioner study and incorporate basic mathematical and geometric structures, Torres-Garcia argued, to ensure a constructivism that will be universally meaningful and understood. In and with these structures and shapes, let the individual develop visual symbols for words and concepts coined by herself, celebrating her own individuality while remaining confident that her individual language remains comprehensible and useful as an artefact of communication.

For the constructive part of this visual language, Torres-Garcia took shapes from the design vocabulary of the Bauhaus and De Stijl movements - in which he integrated what he considered to be personal but universal pictographs, symbols that represent an image or idea, such as a heart or a boat or the sun, the moon and man and woman.

Torres-García believed that the intimate relationship thus produced, between the geometric structure of the plane and its symbolic content, embodied both a personal means of expression & interpersonal dialogue, and an ideal harmony within the universe.

I love offering universal constructivist *paintings and stories* structures – for the powerful affordance they contain, empowering workshop participants to express themselves safely and freely, yet understandably and coherently, and in such a way that dialogue and cooperative learning naturally emerge.

It keeps baffling me how creative and inventive people really are – once the constraints and imperatives of 'being professional' are lifted and freedom is granted to wander into the unknown.

La Ciudad sin Nombre, 1941
universal constructivist visual language by Joaquín Torres-Garcia
photo taken at Museo Taller Torres-Garcia, Montevideo, Uruguay

RESOURCEFUL EXFORMATION

a universal constructivist storyboard
tessellations in an Instagram grid: a Storyboard & Stories workshop
Bayt al-Andalus, Antwerpen, Belgium, January 2020

structures with shape

Perhaps you are like me. When I walk around in a museum, or in someone's house, anywhere at all really, I have this constant urge to touch everything and feel and follow contours and shapes with my hands and my fingers.

Or I feel an overpowering impulse to reach out and take up and gently hold objects against my cheek, searching for an altogether different kind of sensory experience.

Try it. Feel a pebble, washed and polished by thousands of years of waves rolling by - and roll it in your hands and down your cheeks and *become one* with its smooth surface and its temperature, always cooler or hotter than expected.

You must be like me. Because people are notorious touchers.

This can be seen when observing children in a park or a forest or a house or a classroom or the proverbial china shop. This can be heard by overhearing the constant buzz of parental *don't-touch-thats* and *put-that-downs*.

Humans are touchers – and it is by touching that we get to explore the unknowns of the world and the possibilities they incarnate.

Yes, precisely, it is on account of us being a species of touchers, that exformative learning is so full of using objects and things.

In this, objects can be touched and felt for the sake of exploring the objects themselves, like boxes and machines and screwdrivers and sculptures and lawnmowers. But touching an object can also be a ritual act, some sort of baptism, through which the object is endowed with a newly attributed value or meaning - transforming the object into a placeholder of, or a metaphor for, something else - perhaps just an idea or a thought.

Check out, for instance, the ornamental box pictured on the next page. At first sight, just another glass box, mold-blown, with some kind of delicate design. But look once more. This is not just your umpteenth glass box. It has silver and gold and platinum leaf worked into it - and the design makes us think of Taketori Monogatari - the Tale of the Bamboo Cutter, a prominent theme in Japanese folk literature. In fact, this box is a piece of intricate work by Kyohei Fujita (1921-2004), a respected and highly skilled craftsperson, who devoted a lifetime making valuable household objects, with a dedication almost entirely lost in our days. The box is on display at MOMAT, the National Museum of Modern Art, Crafts Gallery, on Daikancho Dori, Chiyoda, Tokyo. The box is priceless. It is behind glass. It cannot be touched.

But wouldn't you want to touch it? Feel it? Isn't it really there to be touched and felt? Have you ever had this texture of alternating glass and precious metals under your fingers? Do you know about the difference in glow and the balance in temperature expressed in the rhythmic patterns of alternating glass and silver and gold and platinum?

Surely, we could learn an extreme lot – with, from and among each other – if an exformative learning facilitator would offer us structures with an inbuilt affordance for touch and feel, and exploration of each other's sensations, experiences and stories.

But this is not entirely the point – at least not necessarily. With the same ease, we could touch and feel the box and attribute any other meaning to it, let us say a cat. We could literally boxify the cat or cattify the box, we could make the box represent the cat or the cat represent the box. We could use the box/cat alliance as a learning or mnemonic device for anything at all – like when we used to tie a knot in our handkerchief in order to not forget to let the cat out in the morning or remember to prepare our toddler daughter's bento box for school.

Objects, objectification, object attribution, or the attribution of (a temporary) meaning to objects – whichever way one turns this, we are left with extremely powerful exformative learning structures.

I even like the idea that the objectification of a certain subject seems to subjectify the object, but might in the end objectify the subject in such a way that the subject ceases to be subjective and turns into a new, objective possibility.

Hm, … I think you should read that last sentence again :-)

*playing with objects,
recreating the history and key ideas of the Agile movement,
exploring possibilities (combining a planar structure with objectification)
at an Agile workshop with Tobias Mayer
42 Acres, Shoreditch, London, UK, November 2019*

structures in time

It is every facilitator's nightmare to not know what to do or what structures to offer at any given moment in the learning process.

If this is your plight – then remember that the exformative learning facilitator is free to offer relevant structures and combine them and create something new at any time – together with the participants.

Just make sure to always take care that with each structure, an identifiable learning value increment is delivered.

Sometimes, the addition of time-related aspects to a structure proves to be a liberating force of its own.

I have learned the deeper meaning of this the hard way, while spending time with patients in waiting rooms of an oncology ward – and seeing how the mere idea of time being finite liberates the powers of joy, contentment and peace of mind.

Another example, on a somewhat lighter footing, is the rule of timeboxing events – for instance in Scrum or in the Lipmanowicz and McCandless *Liberating Structures* we have discussed before.

Likewise, time is often a factor of play – or better, time itself is a player, and we should take good care to allow Mrs. Time to take her due place and play her role and take up her responsibilities in the learning process.

The main implication of adding time to a structure, is that time is an irreversible arrow, creating conditions of expression quite unlike those being at stake when working with purely spatial or planar or shaped-related structures. Takt and beat and rhythm go onwards and onwards and lead us through time in a very particular, almost always unexpected way.

To enlarge this idea, and make it observable, in an embodied way, I sometimes assign workshop participants to create beats while they perform an activity or memorize stuff or while they learn or communicate ideas.

There is a whole world of difference between a sentence loosely said and a sentence contained in a beat, metronomically moving forward.

Metronomes, bells, cymbals and hand drums have been my constant companions ever since I got into the field of facilitation. All provide a sense of proceeding time during whatever it is that we do, creating an embodied echo - and kicking forward our keenness to explore the unknown, perhaps replacing it by a staggering desire to have been exploring as much as possible *before time runs out.*

*storytelling with beats on a hand drum
ikigai workshop with HRD Academy
Koningsteen, Oxdonk, Belgium, November 2019*

word structures

Most structures, but not all, will eventually lead to structures of word.

This is because many of the structural forms I have discussed above, are meant to be temporary placeholders, offered in order to keep possibilities or concepts or ideas in place for a certain time – with the ultimate aim to be a gateway, a medium, by which stories will emerge and will be told, which would remain out-of-reach or would not get to being told, if the placeholders and their gateway function would have remained absent.

And not just the stories - even the individual words of the stories being told would have less meaning if they wouldn't first be made to traverse the medium of other, non-verbal structures.

To understand this, we need to remember that exformative learning is a continuously flowing meaning and value creating process. The structures, that help learners cover distance into the unknown, create meaning and value of their own - and even if nothing at all would happen thereafter, the stream of learning value increments would continue to flow without interruption. Words and verbal expressions are merely yet another value increment.

But there is more. We must keep in mind that the very idea of exformative learning implies cooperation and exchange. We are learning *with, from and among each other* - and therefore, our verbal structures will always be conversational. They involve a number of participants in a cooperatve learning process, each individual taking up the responsibility to contribute to dialogues, trialogues, or any of the many other possible conversational constellations.

Solid exformative verbal structures, being nurtured in a nourishing compost of invitation and voluntary participation, and being grown with the aid of placeholder structures, of space, plane, shape and time, are uniquely meant to be co-practised and co-created.

The cooperative aspect, existing at the opposite end of mere teacher-to-learner transmission of information, represents the very essence of exformation.

For good reasons, therefore, the exformative facilitator should take good care that the very act of verbalisation, the putting into words, of whatever idea or story is at hand, does not cause a collapse of the exformative learning process into mere transmission of information.

In order to avoid the *collapse of exformation* syndrome, it helps at all times to remain mindful of conversational reciprocity.

The idea of reciprocity is easily explained: a continuous, mutual flow of give and take. But practise reciprocity and you will see: it is arduous and testing. It means that in a conversational pattern, every story, every line, yes, every word is at the same time mindfully offered and received – and every offering is a real-time, ad hoc creation, responsive to what came before.

Like thoughts themselves, the words and sentences in which they are packaged, should be seen as presents being exchanged. The gift I have in store for the recipient is both a gift reflecting my own personal preference, choice or contribution - and an offering driven by my sense of empathy, my desire to bestow on the receiver something that might perhaps surprise, but will ultimately please her.

From the recipient's side, receiving the present of a word is both exciting and deeply transformational.

Exciting, because the recipient anticipates that the one presenting the gift is doing so with the aim of offering something pleasing, perhaps something that he had always wanted or that he had expressed a desire for earlier.

Transformational, because the gift has not just a literal value, but a symbolic one on top. Apart from being pleasurable and pleasing, it represents the identity and the personal preference and choice of the giver, or it is something that is so pleasing to the giver that she wants the receiver to experience the same pleasure. Perhaps, and this is crucial, the giver sends out the kind of gift that she would want to receive herself, but the receiver doesn't – and it is up to the latter to reciprocate with the gift of an appropriate but truthful reply.

A slightly unnerving mix of excitement and transformation, or the fear thereof, is a feature of every exchange in our lives – be it an exchange of objects, emotions, or feelings, or a whiz of empathy, or a word or conversation.

Words exchanged remain ambivalent. Words are never final. Merely, they are the onset of something new, a new relationship, an unknown territory of new ideas and possibilities.

*creating real and imagined workplace stories together
a Reimagine Work workshop
Bayt al-Andalus, Belgium, June 2019*

being doubtful

Interestingly, in exformation, it is the qualities of ambivalence and doubt that we are after most of all.

Exformation implies that the practitioner is quite happy with the haziness of words – in fact, she is constantly striving to escape from the realm of the known (information) and go about and roam in spaces of uncertainty, ambiguity and doubt – both structural and existential.

Why would we want learning to be like this?

Because growing in uncertainties, loving how one is enveloped by the veils of doubt, not just coping with, but truly and happily embracing question marks unanswered - is what drives exploration, creativity, innovation, adaptation and improvement.

Indeed: even now, in our century of disruptions and black swans, when people love to name-drop fad words like VUCA and all, and when so many management systems and leadership models and whatnot are claiming to be addressing uncertainty, meeting with one who is truly, abundantly, frolickingly happy with *doubt*, is still a rare event.

Exformative learning is a learning and development method by making things unknown. For this very reason, exformative learning has a tendency of thriving in doubt-driven environments – such as agile frameworks, Toyota's scientific method, or Zen Buddhist monastic practices.

Like those frameworks, exformative learning rests on small iterations and nimble responsiveness to change, temporary hypotheses at all times waiting to be disproved - and acceptance of impermanence (anicca), transience (mono no aware), and the absence of an abiding self (anatta).

the art of being doubtful
a workshop for gentle cooperative facilitators
42 Acres, Shoreditch, London, UK, June 2019

theatrical structures

And look. When space is explored, planes are invaded, shapes discovered, time is trodden and words are being said, what happens?

When games have been played, the child within is unleashed, curiosity liberated, and the whole body transformed into a stage, what happens?

Enters the most complete of artistic expressions, the ultimate game of mankind.

Enters theatre.

Bazeecha-e-atfal hai duniya meray aage, hota hai shab-o-roz tamasha meray aage, once sang Ghalib (1797-1867), famously: The world before me is a children's playground - and endlessly, the play of life is enacted in front of my eyes.

Theatre is everything. It is art, politics and education. It is life. It is exformation.

Theatrical structures are my favourites. Look at how powerful they are, when a whole array of learning value increments has been assembled, now ready for shipping, and one wonders where to go from here.

A theatrical structure often serves as the final packing. It contains review and retrospective, and readies the shipment for transferral to the workplace, the community, the team.

I am an educator, a learning facilitator. I have no formal background in theatre. Instead, I surf.

I surf the waves stirred up by Jerzy Grotowski [22] and and Augusto Boal [23] - creating hybrid learning structures, the kind of which I hope contain affordances for adding surplus value to a workshop.

In most cases, I offer a (very strictly) time-boxed theatrical assignment to a group of participants - who, after a short exformative group conversation, co-create a theatrical piece illustrating a certain idea or learning value increment, in a format comparable to what Grotowski called *poor theatre* - without costumes, props or any theatrical devices.

Facilitators or participants don't need worry about familiarity or non-familiarity with acting, the pieces are the real stuff *para no actores*, to speak with Boal – they are devoid of characters and roles, the participants merely being invited to "play" themselves or an idea they volunteer to express, with our without words.

Ideal is for a group of learners to be divided in break-out groups of no more than ten-or-so individuals – it being difficult to meaningfully include everyone "on stage" in a timeslot as short as the one offered. Normally, I allow just 15 minutes of preparatory conversation and 3 to 5 minutes of acting. When working with bigger groups, the preparation is done by each subgroup in sync with one another, while the plays are presented serially, one after the other.

In theatrical assignments, subgroups are formed with a purpose. For instance, because some of the participants work together at the same physical location, or they work on the same project, or they share a certain this or that (profession, faith, experience, anything) – or because they don't, don't and don't.

The exformative theatrical assignment can go many ways. The facilitator may suggest to create a short theatrical performance or a *tableau vivant* offering an insight into anything at all, according to the context of the workshop. What always works well, is to ask for something that expresses the subgroup's unique added value to the whole, or a feature of the (sum of) the subgroup's self-identified culture(s) - something that differentiates that particular break-out group from the others, or can be considered a gift, or a present, to the organisation, the community, the team.

As for learning context, again, anything goes: the introduction of a new software, how we perceive a certain office ritual, how we envisage our future customer complaint handling routine, how we operate an installation, how we relate as a team to one another in the presence or in the absence of hierarchy.

In theatrical structures, workshop participants are stretched into quick, adaptive, almost childlike creativity. The format urges people to clearly visualize (their views on) matters of key importance to the community of colleagues, the organisation and its stakeholders.

Group members also learn from how the others perform and how the others use creativity to express ideas. I love experimenting with different ways in which to let break-out groups emerge – and seeing how learning outcomes vary accordingly.

Decidedly quirky, yet perhaps the strongest of all learning takeaways, is what Peter Brook, in his preface to Grotowski's book, has called *the shock*.

The shock for the non-actor of confronting herself, in the face of simple irrefutable challenges, evasions, tricks and clichés. The shock of getting a glimpse of one's own learning resources, hitherto left undisclosed, perhaps by lack of a safe space or appropriate structures, or simply because an affordance, however much present and intended by the designer, was unsensed and could not be responded to.

Theatre is a form of knowledge, once said Augusto Boal in one of his legendary workshops, and it should and can also be a means of transforming society. In this sense, exformative theatrical structures can help students young and old to build a future of their own, rather than just waiting for it to be built by those who are perfectly happy with a status-quo or have a path stipulated for others to be walked.

Theatrical structures are not an escape or a refuge, but a medium, a road, a river, a bridge, a pair of wings – providing affordance for the practitioner to truly learn and come to terms with who she is and how she may proceed into the unknown.

rabindrasangeet
singing a Tagore song in a theatrical structure
intercultural workshop at a client's premises
Mechelen, Belgium, November 2019

sociodrama

Sometimes, the shock, referred to by Peter Brook and discussed in the previous section, is so tremendous that a crippling panic occurs.

For sure, the sudden realisation of being released from one's sun-dried chrysalis, comes across as foreboding. Quite naturally, finding oneself equipped with finely textured wings, with which one can fly, can be terrifying. And yet, the liberation represented by both these emotions is one of an exformative theatrical learning structure's great takeaways.

But in order to be able to keep collecting cooperative learning outcomes, the facilitator must keep a fine balance between fear and excitement and curiosity and anticipation – always remaining gentle, always ensuring that participants are not led astray by a sudden disruption of stones having been thrown into the cool and peaceful pool of their mind.

Too much backwash makes a pool unfit for swimming.

Better than to run into disruptive emotional explosions and end up with the participants' inability to keep learning, is for the facilitator to change gear and be somewhat more tight in the theatrical formats she offers - rather opting, perhaps, for the safety of well-researched and widely documented, evidence-based methodologies than the free and naked *let's-see-what-comes-out-of-this* approach that I tend to go for.

Take sociodrama – formerly known as psychodrama.

Like constellations, sociodrama was first used in a context of psychotherapy. The method was essentially developed by Jacob Moreno [24] in the 1940s and 1950s – and has been successfully applied with children and adults, in education and corporate learning, sometimes in a slightly altered format, ever since the turn of the century or even somewhat earlier.

In sociodrama, the workshop participants explore life and

work related situations by acting out emotions and interpersonal interactions – with the facilitator transforming herself into a gentle cooperative stage director. Starting from the story of one of the workshop participants, now called the protagonist, who acts out her story rather than sharing it with words, the group members proceed and act out a number of parallel and alternative scenes, helping the protagonist to work out different scenarios.

The idea is that playing out scenarios, co-construed in small iterations and safely "rehearsed," has a deeper and more lasting learning effect than simply talking through a set of different possibilities.

For the facilitator, practising sociodrama requires gentle stage-directing skills. Combining these with remaining just a facilitator of exformative learning, poses difficulties of its own, and should not be taken lightly.

Sociodrama is a specific structure in time and uses different cooperative formats – none of them easy on the facilitator, while always contributing to liberating insights for the workshop participants, gained with, from and among each other.

an Ulay/Abramowic "silence dialogue"
developing coaching routines in an improvement kata workshop
Koningsteen, Oxdonk, Belgium, September 2019

sociodramatic play

A great deal less formal is sociodramatic play, a concept described and documented by the joint research of Jean Piaget (1896-1980), of *theory of cognitive development* and *genetic epistemology* fame, with Sara Smilansky (1922-2006). [25]

Taken from a context of pre-school education, I first came across sociodramatic play during my years of doing fieldwork with communities of the socially disenfranchised in Bihar, India, in the early 1990s – and I have been working with sociodramatic play structures in adult and even corporate learning ever since.

Sociodramatic play is where workshop attendants act out imaginary situations and stories, become different characters, and pretend they are in different locations and times. As a theatrical structure, it can, but doesn't have to involve the use of props, costumes, and scenery.

To be honest - it works best when nothing whatsoever is used but the participants' sheer imagination.

Often, the introduction of sociodramatic play has a thoroughly unsettling effect on workshop participants. It is fluid, dynamic, and seemingly without purpose. It is self-organizing, cooperative and constantly changes according to the interests and ideas of the players.

I particularly like sociodramatic play, perhaps because it defies any attempt at being categorized as a particular class of play or games or drama.

There are 'at least' (sic) two kinds of games, wrote James P. Carse, in his seminal study of games published in 1986. [26]

A *finite game* is like chess or lacrosse: it is played for the purpose of winning. An *infinite game* is quite something else: it is played for the purpose of continuing the play. Where infinite games are without borders, for finite games, one needs particular boundaries – like a space or a plane and time. In finite games, we play *against* the other or the opposing team. In an infinite game, we need the other to play the game *with*.

While it is certain that sociodramatic play is not a finite game, where actors play against one another with the purpose of winning, it isn't an infinite game either, where all spatial restrictions are lifted – or rather, played with, rather than played along with.

In life, including work, the *infinite game* is *life-including-work* itself. Although sociodramatic play resembles life, it is not equal to life. It is but a temporary exformative structure, allowing the participants to explore and discover possibilities hidden in the unknowns of infiniteness.

Exforming aspects of infiniteness in a finite workshop is nothing short of a real challenge. It needs compromise, and not just a little bit. Typically, I would allow a secretly predefined timeslot for uninterrupted sociodramatic play, providing leeway to freely create and explore new worlds – after which another structure would fulfill the always present need for review and retrospective.

Learnings taken from a workshop's open space of sociodramatic play, have a tendency to be profoundly meaningful, and linger on for many years.

And yes, for a facilitator, it can be deeply disturbing to discover that when she did the least, her students learned the most.

*sociodramatic play and dance
flash mob in Montevideo, Uruguay, December 2019*

experiential learning

So - what does the exformative learning facilitator do? What does the exformative learning facilitator provide, apart from gentle, cooperative facilitation - apart from readying the soil with affordances for structures of liberation from the already known?

It has been suggested for many years now, in both the fields of pedagogy and andragogy, that human beings learn best by doing.

Learning is activity, is a common motto – like when a child sets out into the fields and runs and jumps and moves and laughs.

The facilitator is there only to ready the stage for an atmosphere of creative activity – and is either wholly transparent, absent (?), or a companion in the game being played out.

The difference between cutting and tearing is a thousand strips of paper being cut or being torn. The facilitator ensures the strips of paper to be at hand – and does or doesn't join in on the cutting and tearing, merrily, and verily.

But wait. Experiential learning (EXL or XL) is not just the process of *learning through the experience of doing*.

For *learning* to happen, *learning by doing*, is entirely besides the point. Merely *doing* lacks a structure, and with this, a sense of abstraction – while it is precisely in the realm of abstraction that the wonders of exformative learning take place.

Learning by doing is often not learning at all, or it is learning it wrong by doing it wrong.

It is not *learning by doing* that works so well. It is *learning by reflecting on doing*.

When I was young and just about starting my wanderings in the field of learning and education, the finer implication of this was difficult for me to grasp. Why would practice not deliver results? Why couldn't I just play and play and play Bach's Invention so-and-so – and play it again, until I had it all perfectly right?

I lacked abstraction. I was stuck in one-directional information, contained in the sheet music. I was short of exformative dynamics.

It wasn't until I was a bit older that I discovered the Japanese *shu-ha-ri* tradition and I understood that activity, even in its least formal guise, needs a structure of abstraction to turn it into a genuine learning process.

The shuhari concept was first presented in the Tao of Tea - and quickly made its way into other areas, notably theatre and music, where it was its adoption by the aesthetician, actor and playwright Kanze Motokiyo (1363-1443) that helped it spread.

Roughly, the three syllables describe different levels of balance between abstraction and (manual) practice.

In Shu (守), "protect", the practitioner is meant to focus entirely on transmitted skill and wisdom. The apprentice spends the first timebox of her life as a craftsperson in intent observation, watching the sensei's each and every move, reviewing and retrospecting, but not actively *doing* anything at all. We should not mistake this for an informative learning process, in which existing fundamentals and heuristics are transmitted from A to B. In fact, Shu is a silent dialogue - with both the sensei and the apprentice mentally preparing for the next stage, continuously looking for synchronicity with each other, in a decidedly exformative learning journey.

Ha (破), "detach" or "digress", is exformation proper—where things are made unknown, practices unboxed, traditions questioned and broken with, and the illusion of permanence is shaken off. The apprentice is now actively learning by doing and learning by reflection on doing – through structures and in conversation with the sensei and with his peers.

The last stage is Ri (離), "leave", "separate", the infinite game of life-including-work, where all moves are natural, without clinging to formalism, and transcending the boundaries of physical appearances.

In shuhari, learning is not so much seen as a *learning by doing*, but rather as *learning by experience and reflection* – where *experience* is a product of time and life and skills and peace-of-mind. In a very profound way, shuhari adds a new dimension to Aristotle's observation, done in 350 BCE, in the Nicomachean Ethics, that *the things we have to learn before we can do them, we learn by doing them* – without contradicting the Aristotelean baseline in essence.

In the words of Rabindranath Tagore, an exformative learning facilitator starts by helping us gaze upon earth with utter intent (Shu), when we run forward at full speed, our eyes gazing in front of us, and we see nothing at either side of us. [27]

Next, we need to be shown a door - giving leeway to the unknown, where we can drape ourselves in garbs of uncertainty and doubt (Ha), for, in the longer run, *if things did not move on and vanish, we should see no beauty anywhere* – and *if youth had only the heat of movement, it would get parched and withered, but there is ever the hidden tear, which keeps it fresh.*

In the end, we are forever embracing the unknown and are ready to pursue new pathways (Ri). No longer *the cry of the world is "I have!"* - which was the motto on the coat of arms of information and status quo. Henceforth, *the cry of the world is "I give"* – expressing the idea that exformation cannot exist outside a cooperative space of learning with, from and among one another.

Exformation is an expression of what Tagore calls *the marital bond* between *have* and *give* - an active exploration of reciprocity, deeply engaged and dazzled by curiosity.

In essence, exformative learning is experiential learning with a shuhari twist.

tea with fan and words
tableau vivant at a gentle cooperative facilitation workshop
42 Acres, Shoreditch, London, UK, June 2019

exformation and coaching

brief history of exformation

When the Japanese designer Kenya Hara first proposed the concept of exformation, to his students at the Hara Seminar, Department of Science & Design, Musashino Art University, he had in mind to co-develop with them a novel method of communicating through design – a communication method by making things unknown. [28]

Intrinsically, knowledge is merely the entrance to thought, writes Hara, and *to know things is where the journey of imagination starts, not the goal.*

I fell in love with this even before I read more of it.

At once, I recognised the possibilities of this concept when applied to the world of learning and development, a world in which I had roamed for four decades, in India and Europe and the Middle East - sometimes being *exformative* without even knowing that a word of that order existed.

From early on in my career, three of my main sources of constant inspiration have been Rabindranath Tagore, Paulo Freire and Augusto Boal.

From Tagore I took the use of poetry and painting and play and drama, and it was he who opened my eyes with the concept of *natural learning* - an approach by which we emulate the unartificial and seemingly random way in which a child of less than about 30 months seems to self-develop its resourcefulness. If an optimum learning style exists at all, surely it is this.

From Freire came the idea that this optimum of learning thrives best on a gentle, cooperative process - and from the same source I gained the strong and simple but deeply meaningful insight that true natural learning means liberation.

From Boal, I took the gist of working with non-actors, and the audacity of acting and non-acting with and among them, in a learning context aimed at treading into the unknown – a practice that helped me discover the mind-blowing possibilities of theatrical outsider art, scenic visualisations and conceptual *art brut*.

For all the years since I have been 'touched' by Tagore, Freire and Boal, I have been wildly experimenting with their teachings, turning the chairs around at every failure, and always finding a pomise of light in yet a next step on my own facilitator's road.

Apart from fieldwork with the downtrodden and the structurally and economically disadvantaged, I have worked in areas as different in style and circumstance as education, adult learning, NGO's, telecom start-ups, finance, IT and manufacturing.

And look. So far, I haven't come across a single situation where exformative learning was not at least part of the answer.

in a window piece by James Turrell
Chichu Art Museum, Naoshima, Japan, August 2018

exformative learning facilitation

What, then, are the key features of exformative learning design and learning facilitation?

Exformative learning design implies that a learning process embraces a trajectory that leads into the unknown, and that the unknown can be given value and meaning by the learner herself – in short iterations, always changing and evolving, in sync with the learner's growing resourcefulness and enhancing ability for creative expression of fresh ideas.

We have learned that human beings are naturally talented for exformative learning, but less so as they age - probably because of the restrictive nature of being subjected to a semi-continuous stream of information, or, as Freire would have it, because of the inherently oppressive nature of informative education.

In order for people to rediscover their talent for exformative learning, the exformative learning facilitator exhibits the practice of steady invitation, prodding the learner into voluntary participation in a series of well-designed structures.

Each one of the structures proposed has an embedded affordance for participation, learning, co-facilitation, liberation and an accumulation of insights and resourcefulness.

Think with the mindset of others, Hara tells his students at Musashina Art University. [29] But this doesn't mean having someone else come up with all the ideas for you. It means that, because product design is a practice predicated on universality, it is important to ask oneself how all the others feel and see things – rather than just yourself.

Learning design is very much like product design.

Learning exists in activities and relationships that learners have with one another and with their environment. For this reason, the structures put forward by the facilitator are in essence placeholders for cooperative activities and relationships

– and the more diverse the relationships and the environment in which learning structures are played out, the more successful the learning outcome for every individual structure and the overall learning program will be.

With this in mind, the facilitator plays a gentle game, keenly observing when and where and how affordances are successful and when and where and why they are not – and always on guard to change the design of the learning track accordingly, in real time.

Thus, the facilitator ensures that the learner experiences a steady flow of meaning and of learning value increments, causing the process to roll on and roll forward, empowered by the energy of self-generated motivation.

RESOURCEFUL EXFORMATION

affordance

cooperative facilitation

learning with, from and among each other

retrospectives

reviews

learning structures

no hierarchy

this is that is

making things unknown

a learning collective

coaching

Look at the previous page. Contemplate the basic features of exformative learning facilitation.

There can be little doubt that the exformative learning process, by reason of its focus on group cooperation, cooperative facilitation and complete lack of hierarchy, is a process intrinsically unfit for one-on-one coaching.

The most widely accepted view on personal coaching holds that coaching is a form of development practice, in which an experienced person, called a coach, supports a learner in achieving a specific personal or professional goal by providing training and guidance.

By all means, this definition seems to describe a decidedly unwholesome relationship.

Personal coaching carries the cumbersome weight of an inherent hierarchy, not just of status and position, but also by making use of an informative conversational pattern, with one on the providing side, and another on the receiving side of an information seesaw.

Other approaches present the coach as an appointed mentor, one who is left in charge and guards and protects a less-experienced colleague, sharing knowledge and imparting wisdom in the process – like the old Mentor himself, whom Odysseus left at the side of his son Telemachus, when he strapped his boots for the Trojan War.

Admittedly, over the last few decades, many more views on coaching have been proposed, where the coach is closer to being a facilitator, one who makes things easier, one who is invited, one who is inviting voluntary participation, and one who asks questions but gives no answers.

And yet - even facilitation can be exformative only if it is done collectively and with groups of learners interacting with each other – if the exformative learning facilitator holds the space and offers structures with affordance for the collective to self-organize a cooperatively facilitated learning process.

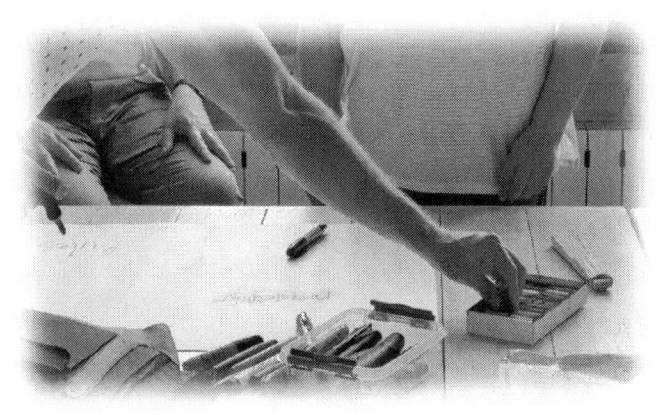

exformative facilitation workshop with (mainly) Scrum Masters hosted by Tobias Mayer at 42 Acres, Shoreditch, London, June 2019

exformative coaching

Imagine an exformative coaching practice. Where clients and facilitators mingle - in groups focused on the cooperative exploration of possibilities present in the systemic whole, but as yet undisclosed. Where people find strength in unknowns and pleasure in uncertainties. Where group members wholeheartedly engage in activities and relationships that will strengthen their own peace of mind, reawaken their resourcefulness, and contribute to the connectivity of the community at large.

Coaching is no longer a form of development practice, in which an experienced person, called a coach, supports a learner in achieving a specific personal or professional goal by providing training and guidance.

Coaching, now, is a cooperative practice of groups of people, in which all the members contribute as co-facilitators, making it easier for all to develop resourcefulness, for the benefit of both the individual and the community in which she exists and interacts.

Coaching, in other words, is what we have been referring to in the previous pages as *exformative learning facilitation*.

生きがいについて / *ikigai-ni-tsuite*
the meaning of life, coaching workshop, Gent, Belgium, February 2019

exformation and vocational coaching

Now imagine the shop floor, the *gemba*, the production line, with operators and team leads. Or think of a development team practising paired programming, or a horse-riding learning track, or an art or crafts class typically set up with a master and one or more apprentices.

Here, the activity of coaching is understood as a kind of vocational training – often aimed at the aspiring operator, developer, equestrian, painter, potter or glass-blower, taking over, no, surpassing the mastery of the role model, who, for all practical purposes, is perceived as being a tutor, trainer, coach or mentor all-in-one.

Considering the kind of vocational training and coaching as practised at the workplace, I cannot but remember the Zen practices of old - the monastic learning routines that I have discovered and practised and learned to love so much in my formative years.

I do realise it may sound dumbfounding to someone unfamiliar with the ins and outs of (Buddhist) monastic discipline, but becoming a monk is very much like learning a trade – and being a novice in a monastery is not in the least unlike being an apprentice in a craftsperson's workshop or at a manufacturing plant's production line.

I know I have been blessed – having been able to spend so many years of my life travelling and doing fieldwork, while always finding enough opportunities to take somewhat long breaks, or rather, study and learning retreats, in an assortment of monasteries, mainly (but not all) Buddhist.

To add to my fortunes, in the second half of the 1980s I was brought into contact with the late Myokyo-ni, born Irmgard Schlögl, 1921-2007, who was a Rinzai Zen teacher in London at the time – and of whom I had the pleasure and the honour of being commissioned to annotate and translate into Dutch a delightful little book about Zen practices, which would turn out to be her best remembered written work. [30]

It was with Myokyo-ni, and through her practice, that I started really researching the non-conventional learning and coaching methods used in a (Zen) monastic context. At first, even to me, these seemed extremely odd, not to say far off, and very contradictory to everything I had learned so far (about natural learning being the best learning framework and structures of play and drama being the favoured boxes from which to unbox the captured mind).

It wasn't until quite a bit later that I became familiar with altogether different Japanese organisational topographies and their respective approaches to the development of individuals and teams – not in monasteries this time, but in industries and production plants – and it was there that I realised how strongly the learning frameworks of TPS (Toyota Production Sytems) and related philosophies are rooted in the same tradition, originally monastic, profoundly liberating, and essentially exformative.

mirror routines with bamboo rods
Toyota Coaching Kata workshop, Beervelde, Belgium, December 2018

kata

In fact, it turns out that Toyota uses *kata*, a word that translates best as *routines*, to ensure the continuous nurturing of a learning spirit in the organisation.

As it happens, the concept of *kata* is firmly rooted in Japanese tradition, more specifically in Japanese martial arts – and was, together with so much more, swiftly absorbed into Buddhist practise from the time of its arrival on the archipelago.

In Zen, for instance, the practitioner engages in routines that help him empty the mind of collateral thoughts, which are considered wasteful artefacts preventing the practitioner to reach the true nature of her mind.

These routines cover every aspect of daily life: from how to put down a pair of chopsticks to how to rinse a bowl, from how to wrench a floor cloth to how to fold a robe, from how to sit to how to breath and how to speak. For everything and everything and everything, it is believed that if only one could manage to keep up the precise routine, the activity would get unburdened from its unwholesome accompanying thoughts and emotions – leaving the mind absolutely liberated from informative noise, and ultimately free.

This is really not just very LEAN – this is no-kidding exformation stuff, isn't it?

koan

Focusing on practical routines, Rinzai Zen, one of the main monastic schools in Japan, has gained a strong reputation for the emphasis it places on the phenomenon of *kensho,* the exploration and discovery of the true nature of the human self.

The idea of *kensho* not only contains the seeds for what we know today as the *leanification* of waste. More importantly, it is this *leanification* that opens up the path to the unknown beyond, the realisation of the true self, the non-self, perhaps, or whatever it is that will be found there - *exformatively*.

Famously, Rinzai training involves *zazen* or seated meditation, and *samu* or mindful daily work performed as a *kata* or routine.

A third distinctive feature of Rinzai training is *koan*, a word used for paradoxes and riddles that have no real answer – often ingenious word plays of unfamiliar logic, turning supposed knowns into unknowns, turning information into exformation.

One day, as Manjushri sat outside the gate, the Buddha inquired:
"Manjushri, why don't you come in?"
Manjushri didn't look up.
"I do not see myself as outside," he said, "why enter?"

Working with koan structures, however, is not easy.

In practice, in a non-monastic context, the exformative facilitator or coach will find it easier to work with metaphors, like *You are a Workmate!* or *My work is a pot!* or *Scrum is an ironing board!* [31]

Koanic and metaphoric structures can be combined with any of the structure formats we have discussed before. For instance, operators in a production plant can be assigned to draw out a personally chosen metaphor of a certain installation unit, after which the drawings are shuffled and randomly redistributed among the participants. In the next round, each operator discusses the installation unit, using the metaphoric drawing of an unknown colleague as an operator's manual.

In whatever form or combination, the purpose of working with koanic or metaphoric structures is to prepare the mind to let go of its informative limitations and boundaries – and rediscover *the pure and true self* of the installation or activity or skill or handicraft of which mastership is required.

RESOURCEFUL EXFORMATION

*improvement and coaching kata
at a rice mill in Belgium, November 2018*

improvement kata, coaching kata

If this sounds weird, do not run away. Working with kata proper is generally perceived as working safely within the realms of common sense and reason.

Toyota has two kata in particular: an improvement kata and a coaching kata – both of them meticulously described and analysed by Mike Rother [32], in the footsteps of whom a worldwide Kata movement and an active community of enthusiast practitioners have emerged.

The first of Toyota's kata, the improvement kata, consists of a very specific structure of learning and improvement, uniquely adapted to complex environments with loads of uncertainties at play - a structure offering affordance for the learner to practise intent observation and scientific research along the lines of Deming's well-known PDCA cycle (plan, do, check, adapt), with hypotheses waiting to be disproved - in short iterations, exploring the unknown, while delivering a steady flow of learning value increments.

The second Toyota kata is the coaching kata, which is in fact a kata for teaching the improvement kata. It consists of a dedicated pattern for a persistent *mentor/mentee* dialogue, which is, as Rother asserts, taken directly from the Zen Buddhist *master/apprentice* blueprint.

Rother describes the kata at Toyota as late to have been discovered by non-Toyota observers, basically on account of their being what they are, that is, underlying routines – and routines, if built-in and practised well, appear so straightforward and natural that even the most zestful of practitioners will have a hard time recognizing and identifying them.

I do not know if the choice of the *mentor/mentee* terminology is Rother's or not, but it will not come as a surprise that it is not the vocabulary that I would have chosen to describe the relationship.

In the coaching kata, it is the *coachee* or *mentee*, and not the coach or mentor, who is the driver of the process.

No questions should be asked, and no answers are ever provided by another than oneself: everything is directed at the *coachee* or *mentee* learning how to ask questions and coming up with (always provisional) answers or performing experiments herself.

The coach or mentor, basically, is like an empty chair, or a mirror – precisely the structural props that are useful to practise imaginary conversations with, and provide a structure for the learner to feel, no, to "dig" the heartbeat of a gentle conversational pattern.

What or who is facilitating what or whom? – The set-up is one of people facilitating one another, in a distinctively exformative learning process.

What is the current situation, what is the current condition (of the system)?
What could be a next target condition?
Which is a next step I could take?
What do I expect will happen if that step is taken?
What withholds me from doing an experiment?
What has happened in the experiment?
How does what has happened differ from what I expected?
What have I learned?
What am I learning?

The questions go on and on.

Answers given are considered unwholesome.

Instead, it is *insights gained* that matter.

It is clear that, in essence, the coaching kata describes a work model for co-facilitated, cooperative, exformative learning.

The cooperative aspect of the coaching kata is built-in and guaranteed by the Toyota overall philosophy that everybody in the organisation is at the same time *mentor* and *mentee*, or *coach* and *coachee* – so much so that it can be imagined that A is a mentor to

B, while at the same time, B is a mentor to A.

Apart from the obvious exformative advantages, the Toyota *mentor/mentee* approach has a wide array of benefits. Peers are in a position of being able to constantly discern how each one of them is thinking and how next experiments are being decided upon or what skills each one of them needs to develop in order to improve, as an individual in her craft, or as a member of the team.

Coach, coachee. Mentor, mentee. I would rather get rid of the words - and simply go for *exformative learning buddy*.

And how intruiged am I - by how the *coaching kata* is operating firmly at the left side of the Agile Manifesto – more relying on people and interactions, stuff that works, *learning buddy* collaboration and responsiveness to change, in the system itself and in the relationships it is sustained by, ..., than on prescribed processes and tools, comprehensive documentation (information), negotiation on roles and responsibilities, and following an outstanding plan. [33]

On top of all this, learning with the improvement and coaching kata requires almost no classroom training, being perfectly suited for learning on the job.

In fact, what Mike Rother is describing in Toyota Kata looks like a pretty strong foundation for a genuine exformative learning organisation.

RESOURCEFUL EXFORMATION

exformation with glass
Peter Kuchinke at The Glass Factory, Emmaboda, Sweden, July 2019

the learning organisation

the koan of exformation

So here we are. We have discussed exformative thinking. We have described matters of exformative learning design. We have dissected exformative learning facilitation and its related structures. We have pondered over the possibility of coaching as an exformative activity.

Now do we know what exformation really is - in the context of the development of resourcefulness in people?

Can we define it?

I don't really know if we can and I don't really know if we should. I don't even know if we should even try.

How much sense is there in defining something, anything, in an exformative way?

Defining something, anything, doesn't come across too strongly as the inherently exformative thing to do.

In exformation, our practice is making things unknown, it is moving from the known to the unknown, from definition to unfinition.

And unfinition, quite literally, is something without end.

As logic would have it, *if we know that 'definition' is an unexformative attribute, then, in order to apply exformation, we should unknow this very knowledge.*

Thus, we have come to the koan of exformation:

By the very act of knowing exformation, we are turning exformation into information – and if we want to turn information back into exformation, we have to know how to unknow.

Know how to unknow, which needs to be unknown.

the art of definition

In exformation, definitions must be open, creative, fluid. Open, creative and fluid definitions are unfinitions.
I am attempting one or two here:

A genuine **learning organisation** is one that thrives on a continuously learning community of resourceful people, all of whom are persistently invited, on basis of voluntary participation, to cooperatively contribute to the facilitation of learning, through the serial application of relevant learning and coaching structures, featuring affordance for liberation of an information-based status quo and for exformative exploration of the unknown, and hence, for an incessant adaptation of the resourcefulness of the individuals and the collective.

Indeed, unfinitions contain unknowns.

Learning means sourcing the resourcefulness of oneself and the collective, in order to help the resourcefulness of oneself and the collective adapt and evolve – always syncing up with user stories emerging from the now and heading for the unknowns of what comes after.

learning is the natural state

Like communities, organisations are all about people. In order to make them thrive and keep them responsive and adaptive to the ever changing circumstances of the unknown, organisations need to nurture people's natural keenness to learn and grow and respond and adapt and innovate.

People are not resources for processes to be running on. People are the essentials of the organisation, and processes are detected in and from the resourcefulness with which the people proceed, engaging in activities and relationships that form the steady grid on which the community or organisation grows.

It's all about people.

It is all about people – and for people, *learning* is the natural state. The change processes we go through, in the course of our lives, are so radical and so continuous, that *not learning* has never been an option.

How fortunate we are, that evolution has always favoured the learners among us.

All of us start in life like a small black object in a gigantic white room, with myriads of impressions and experiences bouncing off from the surrounding whiteness and rolling back towards us, champions of super-absorption.

We are like a small particle of Anish Kapoor's vantablack S-VIS, in an endless, white space.

The real challenge in life is for us to make sure never to loose this absorptive capacity - and for this, we need communities and organisations that nurture our receptivity and strenghten our resolve to never let go of our true, super-absorptive nature.

The best learners are those of us, who continue to let themselves be shaped and formed by their activities in, and relationships with, the social and physical environment.

Only if we continue to learn, will we remain free of preconceived ideas, of bias and other mental constructs that will be limiting our minds as we go along and proceed in life.

Only if we let go of knowledge and so-called *truths* being instilled upon us, but keep absorbing messages from the unknown, will we be able to truly and profoundly keep learning.

Because learning is the natural state - and not learning is an anomaly brought upon us by the aberrations of our society's negligence - and if not, by its wilful oppression.

*the fragile self at play
sensorial games for home isolation technicians
Zoersel, Belgium, February 2019*

learning is an infinite game

If you must play a game, you cannot play a game.
#jamespcarse

Exformative learning implies the use of temporary structures, sometimes finite games, existing within the constraints of a certain space and time, with certain roles and rules and terms of conduct.

But unlike these finite games, the development of resourcefulness in people, the meta-structure of collective and individual learning, is an infinite game, where the roles and rules and terms of conduct must change during the course of play.

Continuous, adaptive changes in the roles and the rules of play, and the terms of conduct therein, prevent the concept of *winning the game* from arising - and ensure the possibility of everyone to join in the game, at all times.

How I love these Carse quotes:

The rules of a finite game are like the rules of a debate. The rules of an infinite game, like language. The rules of a debate dictate how the debate ends, the rules of language ensure language continues.

Finite players play within boundaries, infinite players play with boundaries.

The learning organisation exists beyond boundaries. The learning organisation proceeds into the unknown. The learning organisation is where a community of people sees no problem in playing finite games on the way, while together weaving the infinite tapestry of life, including work.

agile people

The learning organisation is all about people.

What kind of people? *Resourceful people*, for sure.

Agile people, perhaps, as proposed by Pia-Maria Thorén. [35] [36]

People who are curious and collaborative in their continued attempts to create value and innovative solutions that meet human needs.

People who actively seek diversity, by repeated and warm invitation, and based on voluntary participation – an embrace of diversity understood as everyone's right to be and behave and act differently, without being pressured into assimilation and inclusion – because this is how we learn most from and with and among one another, leaving our knowns behind, and turning them into the unknowns of our belonging together in communities.

People who connect deeply with other people and communities in which we live and work together, to create a culture where human resourcefulness is incessantly nurtured, valued and unleashed.

People who pursue value and meaning in what they do and who they are and in the world, in activities and relationships as well as in rest and the joys of silence, retreat, reflection and contemplation – always having in mind that whatever has value and meaning for oneself, has more than double value and more than double meaning when shared.

People who are keen on seeking out opportunities to experiment and learn and doubt and adapt, thriving in the endless improvement kata of an ever changing environment.

People who promote transparency across communities and teams and organisations, and contribute to trust, mental ownership and self-organisation.

People who are true connectors and facilitators, within the communities to which they belong, but just as much across the space between different communities, always keen on contributing to one systemic whole.

the learning organisation

The learning organisation is about people.

People who embrace resourceful exformation.

Because resourceful exformation seems to be a facilitation method by making the perceived limitations of our resourcefulness unknown.

resourcefulness

Exformation is a communication method by making things unknown. [37]

Resourceful exformation seems to be a facilitation method by making the perceived limitations of our resourcefulness unknown.

exformative gardening
Encounters, by Rob Mulholland
Hannah Peschar Sculpture Garden, Surrey, UK, August 2019

web resources

Exformation is a subject deserving public debate. With this in mind, a Resourceful Exformation web page is waiting for you on the Internet.

For access to this page, or if you feel like contributing, contact the author via www.francislaleman.com

Notes and references

[1] Herman Teirlinck: Vijftien Preliminaire Stellingen, in: Dramatisch Peripatetikon, 1959.
[2] Peter Block: Community: The Structure of Belonging, 2009.
[3] Kenya Hara: Ex-formation, 2015.
[4] www.agilemanifesto.org
[5] I have written on the beauty of the agile valuation system in this long read (2018).
[6] Ichiro Kishimi and Fumitake Koga: The Courage To Be Disliked, a classic on Adlerian psychology, 2013.
[7] My takeaways from art are very much like those listed by Pablo Helguera: Transpedagogy, in: Sam Thorne: Schools, A Recent History of Self-Organized Art Education, 2017. Diametrically opposed to Helguera's is my view on the relationship between art and education, as developed in the remainder of this paragraph.
[8] Bruce Mau and Rem Koolhaas: Small, Medium, Large, Extra-Large, OMA - Office for Metropolitan Architecture Rotterdam, ed. Jennifer Sigler, 1995.
[9] Paulo Freire: Pedagogia do Oprimido, 1968. Pedagogy of the Oppressed, 1970.
[10] Kenya Hara: Ex-formation, 2015.
[11] Ralph Russell (ed.): The Oxford Ghalib, Mirza Asadullah Baig Khan (مرزااسدالله بیگ خان), 1797-1869: Life, Letters and Ghazals, 2003.
[12] Johan Huizinga: Homo Ludens: A Study of the Play-Element in Culture, 1938.
[13] Sivasailam Thiagarajan: Simulation Games by Thiagi, 1993; Framegames by Thiagi, 1996, and many more.
[14] I have written on Tagore's philosophy of education a/o in this Linkedin article (2014).
[15] Paulo Freire: Pedagogia do Oprimido, 1968, Pedagogy of the Oppressed, 1970.
[16] Munshi Premchand: Shatranj Ke Khilari (in Hindi), Shatranj Ki Bazi (in Urdu), 1924.
[17] Rabindranath Tagore: The Post Office. With an Preface by W.B. Yeats, 1914.
[18] Henri Lipmanowicz and Keith McCandless:The Surprising Power of Liberating Structures: Simple Rules to Unleash a Culture of Innovation, 2014.
[19] Augusto Boal: Jogos para atores e não-atores, Games for Actors and Non-Actors, 1992.
[20] J.L. Moreno: The Theatre of Spontaneity, 1947; Sociometry, Experimental Method and the Science of Society: An Approach to a New Political Orientation, 1951 – and many more.

[21] Gunthard Weber (on the approach and the methodology of Bert Hellinger): Zweierlei Glück, 1993.
[22] Jerzy Grotowski: Towards a Poor Theatre, 1968
[23] Augusto Boal: Juegos para actores y no actores, Games for Actors and Non-Actors, 1992
[24] Jacob Moreno: Psychodrama, Volume 1, 1946, Volume 2, 1959.

[25] Leah Shefatya and Sara Smilansky: Facilitating Play: A Medium for Promoting Cognitive, Socio-emotional and Academic Development in Young Children, 1990.

[26] James P. Carse: Finite and Infinite Games, 1986.

[27] verses taken from Rabindranath Tagore: Phalguni, Cycle of Spring, 1917

[28] Kenya Hara: Ex-formation, 2015

[29] Kenya Hara: Afterword, Ex-formation, 2015

[30] Myokyo-ni: The Zen Way, in English 1987, in Japanese 1995, my Dutch translation: Het Pad van Zen, Bzztôh, Den Haag 1997.

[31] this one is courtesy of Tobias Mayer.

[32] Mike Rother: Toyota Kata: Managing People for Improvement, Adaptiveness, and Superior Results, 2010.

[33] agilemanifesto.org, 2001.

[34] James P. Carse: Finite and Infinite Games, 1986.

[35] Pia-Maria Thorén: Agile People: A radical approach for HR and Managers, 2017

[36] what follows is inspired by and patterned on, but not the same as, the Agile People Manifesto, in: Pia-Maria Thorén, with Nico & Elsa Simpson: Agile People Picturebook, 2019

[37] Kenya Hara: Ex-formation, 2015.

celebration

The pages in this little book are a celebration of companionship, friendship and love.

My first thoughts of celebration go to my *animus secundus* Michaela Broeckx. It is through constant dialogue and conversation and co-facilitation with her, that my ideas on ex-formation in learning have evolved into their current state.

As much, I celebrate my comradeship with sparring partners and friends across the globe, most of all George Supreeth in India, who has so kindly accepted to contribute a guest column to these pages, making them all the more worthwhile for all of us.

Also, my thoughts of gratefulness go to the hundreds of families in the villages around Bodhgaya, Bihar, India – for it is with and among them that many of the ideas here discussed first emerged. Learning about the development of resourcefulness in human beings from people such as them, has truly been a great privilege.

Most of all, I thank the thousands of students, young and old, who have contributed to and co-facilitated in my classes and workshops, over the many years of my merrily walking the facilitator's path. It is from them and them only, that I learned the most.

Antwerpen, Montevideo, Buenos Aires,
New Year 2019-2020

Printed in Great Britain
by Amazon